CW01560640

"Go Home You Miners!"

Fen Drayton and the L.S.A

By

Pamela Dearlove

To Marie,
best wishes
Pamela Dearlove

Published 2007 by Pamela Dearlove, Hemingford Abbots

Layout by R A Dearlove

© Pamela Dearlove 2007

All rights reserved. No part of this publication may be reproduced, stored in a retrieval system or transmitted in any form or by any means, mechanical, electronic, photocopying or otherwise without the prior permission of the Publisher

ISBN 978-0-9556678-0-0

Printed and bound in Great Britain
by Parrot Print Ltd. Ramsey, Cambs.

Acknowledgements

There are very many kind people who have made this work possible and to whom I am indebted.

I am particularly grateful to my younger son Richard for his encouragement, support and expertise in various fields, including his computing and artistic skills. Also I thank Bob Burn-Murdoch, Curator of the Norris Museum, who proof read, drew maps and advised and encouraged me. He even appeared to enjoy doing so. I thank my husband for his endless patience and I thank my friend Barbara Russell and Ann Merryfield (my sister) for proof reading, and Bridget Flanagan and Nita Luxford for their publishing advice.

My thanks are due also to Mike Bowyer, Aviation historian; the staff of the Beamish Museum; Blom Aerofilms; Cambridge County Record Office; the Cambridgeshire Collection; Cambridge Central Library; Levitts Partnership; the Society of Friends; the University Library, and the University of Cambridge Unit for Landscape Modelling, for allowing me to reproduce photographs and documents from their collections.

Then I add the names of those who have assisted me in other ways, and all (I hope) of those who so generously and unstintingly gave up their time to help me create as full a picture as possible. They include some whose particularly vivid memories, photograph albums and memorabilia, have provided me with a wealth of information and I feel fortunate to have met them and in so doing, made new friends as well as a book. You will meet them throughout the story.

I offer my thanks to Judith Allen, Anne Bowman née Laverick, Rose Burgess (now deceased), Mrs Burns (now deceased), Bob and Jean Carter, Peter Clarke, Tommy (now deceased) and Alice Collier, John (now deceased) and Enid Cox, Sadie Deyton formerly Mrs John Jobling, Ron Foster, Mrs Gash and Brenda Burton (née Gash), Pip (now deceased) and Barbara Gill, Philip Hamlett, Isla Hannah, Julian Harrop of the Beamish Museum, Margaret Hogan née Kiddle, Alan Hunter, Mary Ingham, Mrs Kent-Ledger, Robin Kiddle, Maurice and Jean Lanchebury, Frank Parish, Ivor Pope, Derek and Jean Robinson, Roger Robinson, John Rolfe, Ian and Edna Ruggles, Virginia Smart née Giddings, Jim, Doris (now deceased), Robert and Val Scutt, Theta Smith née Messenger, Derek Tuck, Jack Wilderspin and Mrs Wilson.

Wherever possible facts and stories have been checked. I apologize if any inaccuracies occur in the text. Also, I have made every effort to trace copyright holders of photographs and pictures used in this book. Where this has failed, I apologize if I have infringed rights.

I have written the book for the families who would like to know that their experiences will not be forgotten.

Pamela Dearlove,
Hemingford Abbots
2007

CONTENTS

"GO HOME YOU MINERS!"
Fen Drayton and the LSA

Introduction
The Unique Experiment

"Folks don't seem to have done much for themselves back there in Fen Drayton", said Mr Watson. "I think I made the right decision when I left to move here". He said this in the Spring of 1974, when he heard that I was about to move to the village of Hemingford Grey in Cambridgeshire. I was then working at his garden centre in the lovely setting of Staunton Harold in Derbyshire.

I was curious to know what he meant by "folks back there" but would have to wait a long time before I knew the answer. He also spoke of a Theta Messenger who had moved from Fen Drayton to Hemingford Grey, to whom I might introduce myself.

Years later, I chose Fen Drayton as my topic for a Landscape dissertation because Mr Watson's comments had drawn my attention to the fact that it had had a rather unusual history. It was Theta Smith, née Messenger, who opened my eyes to a different, almost hidden, world and I was very tempted to be diverted from the path I had set out on, and to learn more about 'the folks'. Several years later again, because of Theta and many people with lots of patience, I am able to let others know about them too and of the way in which their lives, and the lives of people around them, were affected by a unique experiment. Also I am now a little more qualified to express an opinion as to whether Mr Watson made the right decision when he chose to leave that world.

***

"As from the end of March, 1983, the LSA will cease Trading".
 Keith Jobling and Neville Gill, like the other smallholders who had committed themselves to the Land Settlement Association (LSA), heard the news in disbelief. Things had certainly been difficult but this was unexpected. In only three months they would be on their own. What would happen to their homes? Who would market their produce? The

large umbrella would be gone with its back-up and advisers which had been provided ever since their grandfathers began their lives as settlers.

34 years before, their unemployed and destitute grandfathers, Jack Jobling and Bob Carter, had arrived in Fen Drayton from the mining and shipbuilding area of Sunderland. Tim Foster from the mining village of Page Bank arrived with them. They were among the first group of trainee settlers to arrive from County Durham in November 1935, to take part in a "unique experiment". An experiment that offered them the chance to support their families and to gain their self respect. They were embarking on a new way of life as settlers on the land totally unaware of the struggles, the tragedies, and the joys that lay ahead, or of the many people who would be woven into the tapestry of their new lives. Nor could they have foreseen where an experiment, begun with such good intentions, would lead.

The parish of Fen Drayton is situated on the border of Cambridgeshire and the old County of Huntingdonshire. It lies between the River Great Ouse and the Huntingdon to Cambridge Road (A14) now the main route to the port of Felixstowe. Anyone who ventures towards the centre of Fen Drayton by way of Mill Road today, will see that its history has taken a different course from that of its near neighbours Fenstanton and Swavesey. They will notice the uniformity of the semi-detached houses that although plain and modest, sit on land holdings of several acres, many of which contain glasshouses. At the gates of some holdings are signs and placards inviting the public to buy ornamental shrubs and plants, whilst on others market garden crops, including tomatoes and lettuce, are being produced.

Further into the village there are more holdings, for they extend over half of the parish, some contain glasshouses in a state of collapse, leaning over nests and tentacles of weeds, while glassless and neglected plots look like wasteland. Less depressingly, some contain horse paddocks, landscaped gardens, or livestock, while in Oak Tree Road several holdings are covered by a gigantic structure, which outdoes anything elsewhere in the village. They are the outcome of Fen Drayton's special history and of the experiment that took place there.

Map of local places mentioned in this book

Chapter 1
Why an Experiment Began

In the early 1930s Fen Drayton comprised about 60 dwellings including Fen Drayton House, a few farms and cottages, the school, the post office, a shop and the Three Tuns public house. In 1931 its population had shrunk from the 450 recorded in 1861 to about 200. Like many other villages at the time it was in decline and in a sorry state. The waterways into the village were overgrown and boats no longer transported goods into its heart. Abandoned cottages were left to decay and others were almost uninhabitable, as were a row of rundown thatched cottages opposite the Three Tuns. One was home to Pet Lelly a Rag and Bone or Knacker man, another was home to George Ingle, one of a family of seven. He told me that it had no indoor water supply, sanitation or electricity, and that he and his family climbed a ladder to get to bed. Another resident complained in the Cambridge Weekly News in 1936 when the village pump had been out of order for three months. She said that half the village relied on it and "if it should fail completely we do not know what we shall do for water". Isla Hannah née McDermot said her family caught soft rainwater in a zinc bath to wash themselves with.

The northern half of the parish was mainly marsh and pasture while the southern half contained about seven farms, including those of the estate of Fen Drayton House, and market gardens and orchards.

c1934 the aunt and uncle of Isla McDermot (later Hannah) are taking a summer stroll down New Road (now High Street) in Fen Drayton. They are visiting their relatives, Isla's grandparents, who live in the blacksmiths home behind them. The child, Roy Sidney Culpin, is Isla's cousin.

The village was composed mostly of closely interrelated family networks. These included the Johnson and Wilderspin farming families, Mr Hard a smallholder, whose produce included poultry, flowers and plums, and the Smarts, the Giddings, the McDermots, the Culpins, the Burtons, the Ingles. the Parishs and the Greens.

Fen Drayton village school children in 1935
L to r: back row: unknown, Frank Parish of Islip Farm, Ernest Carter, Miss Clarke
Middle row: Norah Lambert, Gwen Johnson, ? Freda Ding, Vera Parish
Front row: Les Ding, Jane Tattershall, ? Marjorie King, Ron Ingle, of High Street, Lily King, Jean Wilderspin
The children aged between four and 11 were all taught together and Frank Parish remembers the teacher had difficulty controlling them.

Villagers who did not work on the farms and could not find other work in the parish travelled to Cambridge, Fenstanton, or St Ives, for employment. In the fruit season some were transported to farms further afield, by the open-topped double-decker bus of Chivers of Histon with its stairs on the outside, to pick fruit to be canned or made into jams or jellies at the Chivers factory.

"A civil inoffensive man", Mr Househam, a Sunday School teacher at the chapel, also delivered milk in the village. In winter, a dewdrop on the tip of his nose was observed apprehensively by his customers as he ladled the milk from a churn which he transported on his bike. Mr Househam was very proud of his two or three cows, which he grazed on grass verges including some near the war memorial in Horse and Gate Street. Other villagers were not so civil. At the Parish Church two successive curates had resigned, "disheartened by the 'cantankerousness' of a faction of parishioners".

James Culpin, blacksmith, and his wife Lydia (Isla Mc Dermot's grandparents), are at the rear of their home in New Road (now High Street). The forge was close by.

During the summer months men played cricket and in winter locals skated on the frozen flooded fenland close to where, for many years, skilled skaters like William "Gutta Percha" See and James" Turkey" Smart competed in thrilling races. But it seems there were few other sources of entertainment in the village.

A world economic crisis followed the 1914 – 1918 war and it became known as the Great Depression. Although the countryside was deeply depressed agriculturally, Fen Drayton's villagers, like a large proportion of the nation, were mostly unaware of the bitter hardship and misery being experienced by unemployed industrial workers. There were newspaper reports of min ers' strikes and lock-outs and occasional radio appeals for funds and help, but the difficulties experienced by people like Jack Jobling, Bob Carter and Tim Foster, away in the north east of England and Thomas Pope in South Wales, who all had no hope of ever finding work, were far remote from their minds, until they were confronted by a unique experiment.

In 1935 the opening of the new cricket pavilion in Fen Drayton was celebrated with a match between teams from Fen Drayton and Swavesey.
L to r: two unknowns, James Culpin (blacksmith), ? Captain Fred Johnson, Joe Green, (publican), Ernie Smart, George Smart, Mr Hard (fruit grower), Fred Wilderspin senior (farmer), unknown, unknown, Eddie Warboys, Sid Wright, Edward Warboys, Gwen Johnson seated, unknown, unknown, unknown, Tom Savage, Bert Gray, three unknowns, Bobby Wright seated, two unknowns, and Arthur Young.
Sid Wright and Tom Savage were from Swavesey.

1936 - "Competition at Skating Championship, Swavesey"
Thrilling races were held for many years on the frozen floodwaters of the Fens. Local people waiting for the races to begin at the Skating Championship event at Swavesey.

1895 - Turkey Smart "Champion of England 1854 – 1859"
"For power and true Fen Stroke he had no equal, and was the fastest Skater, his record has not been beaten, - Uncle to Fish, and James Smart, the Ten Miles Champion Skater". Here photographed with William "Gutta Percha" See (left), who was also a skating champion.

9

The Great Depression

It is hard to comprehend the extent of the misery of people's lives during the years that followed the 1914–1918 War. It seemed there would never be enough work again for those in many industries including shipbuilding and mining. Many disputes between coal miners and mine owners led to the General Strike called by the Trades Union in 1926 and miners already short of work became almost permanently unemployed. In England alone there were nearly 2 ½ million men unemployed by 1931. It is through the stories of individuals we can learn a little of what it was actually like to be an unemployed miner or shipyard worker or to lose one's livelihood because of the widespread unemployment in your neighbourhood.

Durham Hunger March passing through Houghton-le-Spring, 1936. The banner reads "DURHAM, MARCHING AGAINST STARVATION".

Bob Carter, a Sunderland shipyard worker born in 1899, married Ellen Rose, who inherited money from her father, a blacksmith who had worked for the mines. In the early twenties, Ellen Rose encouraged Bob to leave his job at the Tyneside shipyard to start a home-made ice-cream business. He sold "Carter's Ice-cream", some from the promenade near his home, while his wife ran their bakery and grocery shop. But their businesses could not survive the poverty, increased by the General Strike in 1926, and they went bankrupt. Another of their ventures, a sweets and tobacco shop, failed in 1933, again because of the poverty in the district, which also affected the fishermen of the herring fleets who landed their catch on the quayside nearby. These desperately tried to sell herrings at 12 or 14 for a penny, almost giving the fish away. Bob's son Bobby was fortunate to have boots to wear, but other children went barefoot in summer and with only rags wrapped about their feet suffered in the bitterly cold winters.

A father of three, Bob, whose relatives were also suffering the effects of unemployment, cycled miles and miles unsuccessfully in search of work in the mines and shipyards. The family's Bed and Breakfast business, frequented by travelling theatrical groups, helped them to survive.

Bob Carter selling his home made ice cream to a customer on the promenade near Roker, Sunderland. His son Bobby nearly drowned in a tub of ice cream after leaning in too far to taste it, but that is another story.

Jack Jobling, also in Sunderland, was one of the many laid-off shipyard workers too. "He tried everything to get work in the mines and shipyards" and was on the dole for a long period during which tragedy, common at that time, struck the family. I was told that Kenneth, his two year old son died from diphtheria when the doctor failed to recognise the symptoms.

In the mining village of Pagebank, County Durham, lived Tim Foster, who was born in 1900. He was allocated a typical miner's house in a terraced row. It had a lavatory down the yard, "a bucket and chuck it", and was loomed over by an ugly slag heap in which George and Tim junior, two of his young sons, scrabbled for coal to stoke the black kitchen range to heat water for Tim's nightly bath (there were no pithead baths). After a year's work, Tim was back on the dole and found it difficult to feed the family. A small allotment was a godsend as was a soup kitchen, started up to help the redundant workers. Ron said the neighbours "kept their chins up" and "helped each other out". At this time Gracie Fields was warbling "Sing as we Go", the anthem of the Depression. In 1932, penniless and desperate, Tim cycled from Durham to Derbyshire in search of work but turned for home when his new baby son was born. With his bicycle tyre punctured, and no money for repair materials, he had to ride the last 23 miles with the tyre stuffed with grass.

Miners' houses were often unfit to live in. Page Bank was a small mining village near Spennymore, which Ron Foster remembers, looked just as grim as it does in this photograph when he and his brothers left it for Fen Drayton. Most of the houses have since been demolished.

12

Ivor Pope described to me family life with his father Tom born in 1899, who was a miner living in the Welsh valley of the Rhondda. Tom took part in the General Strike of 1926 and lost his job. Infant mortality was high and several of the 13 children his wife bore died young, including twins, and Ineas who died from Diphtheria. Ivor, born in 1920, contracted rickets for which he was made to take brimstone and treacle. With his father he would burrow by candlelight, into the dripping wet Trealaw mountainside to get coal. They dragged out tons, more than strictly allowed, so they could sell it. One day Ivor had a lucky escape when Tom, who had returned from dragging coal to the surface on a sledge, recognised an ominous sound. The tunnel supported by table legs for pit props was collapsing and he yelled to Ivor to run for his life.

1935. On a Rhondda mountainside Tom Pope (dark shirt) sits in the centre of a group of miners who are about to form an allotment co-operative. Yes the allotments will be on the mountainside.

Ivor said anything of value in the home was sold in order to claim the dole. His father also received vouchers for stamps given to him for building new parks for the local council. These were exchanged for goods at the Co-op. Tom encouraged self-help and the family were all adept at make-do and mend. Mrs Pope made clothes out of old overcoats given to her. These were handed down through the children gathering different coloured patches as they went. Tom made the coffin for the twins' funeral and taught the boys to mend shoes, to sew on buttons and to cook. Ivor would rise at 5.00 a.m. to help unload the baker's vans for which he was paid in cakes. His family traditionally on Sundays gathered in the parlour where Tom would play the violin. When it was broken he bartered several bags of coal for a gramophone to which they would all sing along. Tom was also a member of the Treorchy Male Voice Choir. Then, in 1935, when aged fifteen, Ivor left Wales to work for the Home and Colonial Stores in Oxford, while his father formed a co-operative allotment society with other miners to scrape allotments out of the rock-strewn mountain side. But with no hope of paid employment he too decided to leave Wales. He would take up an offer, the offer of a completely new way of life.

Idealism and Philanthropy

Many hearts were touched by the plight of the families of the unemployed, for whom donations were contributed from five continents and 27 countries, while various charitable groups and concerned individuals, including J. Rowntree of the chocolate family, laboured to make the lives of the destitute more bearable. Ivor Pope told me he felt great admiration and gratitude to the Salvation Army in particular, because they gave him and other hungry children on their way to school a cup of cocoa and bread and jam. Among other caring people and organisations were the Quakers (The Society of Friends), who helped thousands living in poverty. They provided clothes and food and renovated old shoes and aided people to help themselves. Most significantly they provided allotments so families could have fresh vegetables, and made available badly needed tools and seeds, providing some to a man who previously had planted the "eyes" from discarded potato peelings. They experimented with so many different types of allotment schemes that they built up a wealth of experience.

Welsh miners managed to grow vegetables on allotments on most unpromising terrain.

By 1934 some men had been out of work for 15 years, and anyone over 35 years of age had little prospect of working again. It was obvious to many that more drastic action was needed, particularly for the older age group.

Among those who thought the solution to unemployment lay in returning men to full-time working on the land to earn their living, was a Mr (later Sir) Percy Malcolm Stewart, of Sandy in Bedfordshire (his home is now the headquarters of the RSPB). Chairman of the London Brick Company, he was a dynamic personality who had founded the model village of Stewartby in Bedfordshire for its workers. In the summer of 1933 he visited Friends' House to ask the Quakers, whose work with allotments he admired, to set up an experimental scheme to which he would donate £25,000 if matched by the Government. The Scheme was to settle unemployed industrial workers on full-time landholdings away from their home areas. A protracted series of meetings followed, between the Quakers, other charitable organisations, and Ramsey MacDonald the Prime Minister. Frustrated by delays Malcolm Stewart spurred the Government into action by buying a 535 acre estate at Potton in Bedfordshire and then writing to Ramsay MacDonald to ask for the Government's £25,000. A committee was formed with representatives from The Society of Friends, The Carnegie Trustees, The National Council of Social Services and interested individuals including Malcolm Stewart.

An Important Announcement

The Land Settlement Association (LSA), was born on 26 July 1934. The Minister of Agriculture announced in the House of Commons that the Association had been formed "to carry out an experimental scheme for the provision of small-holdings for unemployed persons, with financial assistance from the Government". The rules of the Association stated that "The objects of the Association shall be to carry on the business of providing and equipping land for cultivation by unemployed persons or persons in part-time employment and providing training and maintenance for prospective holders and to do all such things as the Association may think conducive to the attainment of the above objects".

Opponents of the scheme, of whom there were many, said earnings would be no more than if the men were on the dole. In their book "Back to the Land" in 1935, C. S. Orwin and W. F. Darke, wrote "there is no more justification for raising the cry of 'back to the land' in the mining villages of Durham or the shipyards of Barrow and the Tyne, than for raising the cry of … 'back to the hand loom,' in Lancashire". But they thought the scheme might perhaps provide a slight alleviation of people's distressing circumstances..

The LSA's Executive Committee was reluctant to begin what seemed a huge task but decided to experiment with just six estates. Then the Government appointed Malcolm Stewart as Chief Commissioner for the Special Areas (England and Wales), areas where unemployment was most deep-seated, including Northumberland and Cumberland, and allocated him money to combat unemployment in them. He then persuaded the LSA to set up enough estates to transfer some 800 families to full-time smallholdings in other parts of the country. (A Welsh Land Settlement Society was created to administer similar schemes in Wales).

Unsuspecting villagers throughout England, including those in Fen Drayton, would soon have their lives affected by this decision

The logo of The Land Settlement Association.

Chapter 2
An evolving estate
1934 – 1939

With little time to design and plan the LSA embarked on the enormous task of creating 24 smallholding estates. These needed the right components to enable miners and shipyard workers to change to a totally new way of earning a living, and a lot of care and supervision would be required for men going from idleness to all-week exertion. To increase the settlers' chances of success, certain principles were considered essential.

Firstly, that the smallholdings should be established in groups around central farms, and organized as administrative units under estate managers; secondly, that training and supervision should be provided for the settlers; thirdly, that cooperative methods should be used to purchase their agricultural requirements and to market their produce; fourthly, that expensive tools and capital equipment should be available for them to hire, and lastly, that loans at favourable rates should be available to aid them to equip their holdings. These principles, never before operated together in a land settlement scheme, were considered vital for its success and also were what made the scheme unique.

Applicants to the new scheme had to be men between 30 and 50 years old who were long-term unemployed, prepared to work hard for long hours and, preferably, to have held an allotment. Their wives had also to be interviewed because they had to agree to support and work alongside their husbands.

The Land Settlement experiment was to begin as quickly as possible. Potton Estate was already available but it was difficult to find others with early vacant possession, which could provide smallholdings that could promise a decent living, and that were close to local social amenities. Conveniently, in 1935, Fen Drayton House Estate was advertised for sale by auction. The owner Mr Evison, who was in his nineties, was retiring to Wales. The Estate, situated in an area with a tradition of smallholdings and market gardening, and conveniently near to road and rail links to national wholesale fruit and vegetable markets, seemed to match the LSA's list of requirements.

Mr Evison outside the Methodist Chapel in Fen Drayton. He sold his Fen Drayton Estate to the LSA and then retired to Wales. The Chapel has since been demolished.

The Estate Agents' Sale Plan of the Estate, described market garden land containing valuable gravel beds, Daintree's Farm with 65 acres of land, Middleton's Farm with 72 acres, Fen Drayton House, 15 cottages, fen pasture land and orchards – in all nearly 350 acres, which was divided into 32 lots. The first four lots were the gravel bearing land.

No doubt prospective bidders at the auction of the Estate, held at the Lion Hotel, Cambridge, on 29 June 1935, were very disappointed to learn that all but the gravel bearing land had already been sold. They heard, so the Cambridge Chronicle reported, that it was unusual to sell land before auction, "but a semi-public body which was concerned with settling families on the land from depressed areas deserved special consideration".

By Direction of John Evison, Esq., J.P.

FEN DRAYTON

Cambridge 9 Miles.   St. Ives 4 Miles.

Particulars, Plan & Conditions of Sale of

MARKET GARDEN LAND

containing

VALUABLE GRAVEL BEDS

DAINTREE'S FARM, 65 Acres

MIDDLETON'S FARM, 72 Acres

FEN DRAYTON HOUSE

15 Cottages

Fen Pasture Land

and

Orchards

MAINLY WITH VACANT POSSESSION

in all nearly

350 Acres

For Sale by Auction in 32 Lots by

Messrs. BIDWELL & SONS

At the LION HOTEL, CAMBRIDGE

On SATURDAY, JUNE 29th, 1935

at 4 p.m.

Solicitors:—SIDNEY J. PETERS, Esq., M.P., LL.D., 25, St. Andrew's Street, Cambridge; and at St. Ives and Huntingdon.

Auctioneers:—Messrs. BIDWELL & SONS, Chartered Surveyors; *Head Office:* 2, King's Parade, Cambridge, and at Ely and Ipswich.

Fen Drayton Estate Sale Document

21

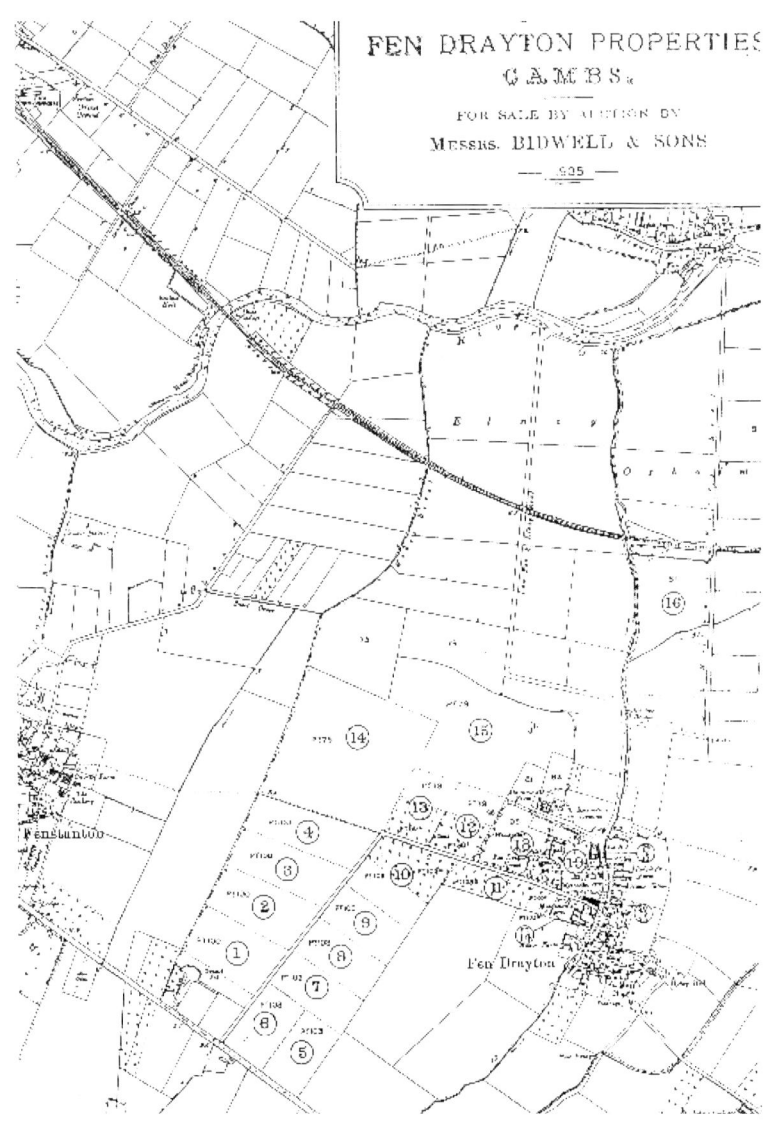

Fen Drayton Estate, which included a large house and two farms, was put up for sale by auction in 1935. The LSA bought all but plots 1 – 4, the gravel bearing land. Shortly afterwards it bought extra acres from a Mr Scambler, to create the Middleton Way holdings.

Although this story concentrates mainly on Fen Drayton's LSA smallholding estate, which was just one of a number of the Association's estates, I should perhaps point out that the full-time smallholding scheme was only one of many schemes administered by the LSA. It was also involved in part-time schemes including group holding allotment schemes, orchards, stock allotments and cottage homesteads.

Fen Drayton House built for Captain Daintree in c1850 by a superior London architect. Its servants' quarters were added at a later date. Mrs McDermot, housekeeper to Mr Evison until he sold the house in 1935, looked after trainees and failed settlers who lived in the house. In later years it accommodated LSA staff.

Settlers Arrive

On the 1 November 1935, the Cambridge Weekly News reported that the first contingent of 40 men for whom the LSA had purchased the land, had arrived in Fen Drayton. The men were from County Durham. In fact ten men had arrived to be followed by a further ten after Christmas. 20 was considered the largest number that could be trained at one time. We have already met Jack Jobling, aged 37, Tim Foster, 35, and Bob Carter, 36. They, with other trainee settlers, were billeted at Fen Drayton House. Among them, from County Durham, were Thomas ("Tot") Collier, from Perkinsville, aged 46 (he was the oldest of the arrivals), and Christopher

23

("Kit") Messenger (former blacksmith to hill farmers and miners) aged 43, from Esh Winning, with his brother Walter, from Waterhouses. They were all looked after by Mrs Mac, (McDermott), housekeeper to the former owner of the house.

Drayton House, as it was once called, was described in 1854 as "a very superior residence which had been built within a few years by an eminent London architect, and furnished with great taste by J. C. Daintree". The principal rooms were described as having "superior" marble chimney pieces. Before 1935 a considerable extension for servants' quarters had been added and the house was able to provide homes for LSA staff, and temporary accommodation for failed settlers. I was told that the marble fireplaces, which were very beautiful, were removed some time after 1946.

Daintree's Farm provided a home and an office for Mr Piper the first Warden of Fen Drayton Estate. Its stables and outbuildings housed equipment and supplies.

With an entrance on Cootes Lane it was set in parkland and ornamental woodland on a modest scale, and had a walled kitchen garden, and a landscaped garden with paths edged with neat box hedges and topiary. Would these survive?

The Estate's properties were quickly adapted by the Association for its use. Daintree's Farm with its stables and outbuildings, was used to house equipment and certain supplies. It also provided a home for the Estate Manager, until the early 1950's. Middleton Farm, and its cottages and barns, became the hub of the whole estate - its Central Farm, acting as a buying and selling centre for the tenants, with grading and packing sheds, piggeries, the estate office, a shop, and storage space. The Central Services were the fundamental part of the Scheme, where services for the settlers could be provided on a large scale so more economically. The farms and their associated buildings became hives of industry creating a new sense of vitality around them.

The settlers were welcomed into this new world by Mr Piper, Fen Drayton Estate's Warden, and Ray Ward his deputy. Mr. Piper, previously Horticultural Manager of the South Eastern Agricultural College at Wye in Kent, had arrived a month earlier to work from a room in Daintree's Farm from where, his daughter told me, he kept rushing to St Ives to get supplies of stationery and office equipment. He, with the aid of a number of experts, was to instruct the trainees in the various types of agriculture, horticulture and animal husbandry, and to organise all the buying and selling for the Estate. As Warden, Mr Piper needed technical knowledge and experience, organising ability, business skills and the gift of leadership. Unsurprisingly, the Association had difficulty in recruiting men with all these desirable qualities. Mr Gammins, a Director of the LSA, was to describe the Warden (later called manager) as the lynch pin of the whole organisation.

After years of unemployment many trainees were physically and psychologically impaired so the first three months of their training was organised to help them get fit and build up their strength. At Fen Drayton they surfaced the muddy tracks of Daintree's Lane and Springhill Road and created Middleton Way and Oak Tree Road, and also the service tracks which were to provide easy access between the holdings and Daintree's and Middleton's Farms. The trainees also cleared the land of orchards in Cootes Lane and divided the estate's fields, with another purchased from Mr Scambler a local farmer, into 54 plots of 3 to 6 acres. 50 holdings were considered necessary to make an estate economically viable. The rectangular plots fronted onto the roads, which included the existing Mill Road and Cootes Lane. It was hard work setting up the estate's infrastructure and Tim Foster missed a visit to Unwins Seeds because he took a break and visited his family. On one such visit he took home a suitcase filled with fruit from the orchards, providing a rare treat for his children.

Early settlers outside Fen Drayton House.
Mr Redhead, Mr Brownson from South Shields, William Laverick from Sunderland, ?Lennie
Robson from South Shields. Front row - unknown, unknown

Trainee settlers from Co. Durham on a visit to Unwins Seeds of Histon in 1936.
L to R:
1. James Brown from Crook, or Mr Clarke
2. Mr Abernethy, Pallion, Sunderland
3. Christopher Messenger, Esh Winning
4. Tony, 'Joby' Nutall, Thornley
5. Tom Collier, Perkinsville
6. John, 'Jack Jobling, Ford Estate, Sunderland
7. Bob Carter, Ford Estate
8. Mr Parr, Newcastle-on-Tyne
9. Albert Crick
10. Edward Stott, Sunderland
11. ? Mr Telfer, N. or S. Shields
12. 'Darkie' Lane (LSA worker)
13. Walter Messenger, Waterhouses
14. Tommy Lumley, village near Esh Winning
15. Scott Finlay
16. Tom Johnson, Spennymore
17. Harry Sawyer, Spennymore
18. Ted Harrison

In "The Fen Drayton Estate of the Land Settlement Association. A Record of 8 years Progress", written in 1943, possibly by Mr Piper, it was explained that the men constructed Fen Drayton's holdings in a particular manner.

"...The Estate Manager's idea was to lay out the smallholdings in such a way that through cultivations could be done in the same manner as on the large mechanised market garden farms. This plan was put into operation and adjacent holdings were planted right through with the same crops. Thus if a batch of ten holdings had one

27

acre each of potatoes, one acre of brassicas and one acre of roots each crop was put in the same place on all the ten holdings thus enabling cultivations on each crop to be carried out right through the ten plots." ...

and that

"Thirty acres of soft fruits were planted in blocks on the holdings in such a way as to facilitate through cultivations as on the large fruit farms. The fruits were gooseberries, blackcurrants, redcurrants and raspberries".

This system caused antagonism between settlers, and they wished to cultivate their holdings individually. Not until some time after the war did they get their wish when the holdings were planted and cultivated separately, thus allowing them some freedom to choose what crops they would grow and where.

The trainees erected piggeries and poultry houses on the smallholdings, and a glasshouse (it became known as the landlord's), a smaller propagating house, and 100 Dutch Lights (cloches). The physical work improved their fitness and soon they were producing crops and selling lettuces of good quality through Covent Garden, and won the prestigious order to supply lettuces for the maiden voyage of the Queen Mary.

Mr Piper, the warden, is supervising Fen Drayton's first trainee settlers. They are packing lettuces for the maiden voyage of the Queen Mary in May 1936. Although the construction of the houses, seen in the background, was delayed by bad weather, it seems it did not affect the settlers' produce. This had already acquired a measure of fame by topping the market for quality and price on more than one occasion at Covent Garden.

They were eligible for the dole until they had proved themselves competent enough to run their own holdings after about 15 to 18 months. This often proved to be over optimistic. During the training period they were given technical instruction on the central farm and on their own holdings. Jack Jobling gained the tenancy of 34 Cootes Lane, Tim Foster of 9 Mill Road and Bob Carter was allocated 25 Springhill Road.

Each holding cost £1,000 to set up. The permanent assets of houses, buildings and land represented £700. £300 was working capital, the amount required to stock the holdings. Some of this was written off by the LSA, and the balance was a loan without interest repayable on easy terms. The settlers paid a rent for the holdings that, it was calculated, would give the state a reasonable return on its money. They were not allowed to buy their holdings because, firstly, should they or their wives prove unsuitable their tenancy could be terminated, and secondly, because it was thought that a further loan to buy the house and land on top of the long-term loan for stock and other equipment, would be too great a burden for them.

The men's families began arriving in 1936. Their travelling arrangements had been organised by the Ministry of Labour. Bob Carter's family from the Ford Estate, Sunderland, caught the train south to be joined by the Collier family at Durham. They were all met at Peterborough Station and driven to Fen Drayton. R. Kiddle and Son, furniture removers of St Ives, had fetched the family's belongings from the north. Aged eleven, Bob Carter's son Bobby's first impression was that Fen Drayton "seemed wonderful - a different world". As he passed the ten plots in Mill Road on the way to Spring Hill, he was delighted to see orchards everywhere and the woodland which was full of bird song.

Because bad weather held up the building programme, Ron Foster said it was 1937 before he, then aged five, and his elder brothers, said goodbye to their friends. They were photographed by the "Northern Echo", which reported that they were leaving for a new life. Tim junior, to his Mum's embarrassment, had put on a "holey" jersey, and there was no time to remedy it.

The family's big adventure began on The Flying Scotsman. Then they were met at Swavesey Station by a Mr Parish. He drove them to where their father stood outside "a lovely, brand new, four bedroomed, red brick house". The boys were soon fighting about who would sleep where, until Mam sorted them out. They had never before seen a bath with running

R. Kiddle & Son's removal van, which carried the furniture of many of the northern settlers to Fen Drayton in the 1930's. Because the van travelled slowly the operation took two days. The removal men would leave St Ives at 5.30 a.m. but would not begin loading the furniture at their destination until about 10.00 p.m. Then the following day, Mr Robin Kiddle said, it was quite usual for the families to undertake the journey south seated on a settee balanced on the van's tailboard.

water, or a lavatory that flushed, and because they were used only to seeing gas lamps in the street, they kept turning the electric lights on and off in great excitement. The water supplied to the houses had been obtained after extensive trials. Ron reckoned it was the "best tasting water he had ever drunk". Bertie Butters, who as Surveyor of Works installed services on the estate, told me the water analyst was not quite so happy about it. He had pronounced it unsuitable for invalids. By June 1937, the Foster family and the Carter and Collier families, were among 37 families embarked on a new way of life on Fen Drayton's LSA Estate.

The Impact on Fen Drayton.

Unlike Potton's villagers who, fearing competition from the new growers, joined protest marches, Fen Drayton's villagers appear to have been less fearful as to what lay in store for them. Nevertheless, they were startled when the strangers arrived for they spoke a foreign language. Like Tot

Collier and his son Tommy, with particularly thick northern accents, the northerners were very difficult to understand. But the locals received early hints that at the least, the sociable northerners would prove to be the source of new interests and entertainments.

As early as 17 January 1936, the "Weekly News" reported:

"Fen Drayton Village School was crowded out in celebration of the arrival of the men from Durham. The miners entertained the villagers with items and choruses which were greatly enjoyed, and the intention was expressed that more such entertainments would follow".

The northerners with their background of Methodism swelled the congregation of the local Chapel. A local resident remembered they had lovely singing voices. The chapel itself also benefited from the new worshippers and was reopened in August 1938, after cleaning and renovation. Sadly it no longer survives. When 20 more men arrived in April, a cricket match was held on Good Friday between villagers and miners. The miners won by two runs.

The small village school, with its non-flushing lavatories, felt the full impact of the arrival of so many new families. Instead of an average of five new pupils being admitted each year, as between 1928 and 1935, 35 children arrived in 1936 and more again in 1937. They came from schools such as the Alwyn, West Hartlepool, and the Crook School and the Blue Coat Schools, Durham, and Botham School, Newcastle, and Seaham Harbour school, Sunderland. A temporary infants' classroom provided extra space at the overcrowded school in 1937, and an extension was added later, but it was not until 1970 that the school moved to newly built premises in Cootes Lane.

Jack Wilderspin, a farmer's son, said he felt intimidated by the northerners who arrived when he was only five years old. He and his schoolmates were totally outnumbered by the newcomers. He was frightened of them even though they were only small because some seemed very rough and would throw stones. Several of their names feature in the school punishment book. Theta Messenger (more of her later) and Alwyn Heath, received one stroke on the seat for the minor misdemeanour of "continuing talking". More seriously, on September 14 1937, Dennis Lumley was caned, after a warning, when a child was knocked over. It seems Fred Telford was having trouble settling in for in September 1938 he was given

31

two strokes of the cane for playing truant for a second time and taking two infants with him. Tim Foster's son George had two strokes on the hand on 21 March 1938, for throwing stones in the playground, and again on 3rd February in 1939, for inattention and bad work. On 17 November 1939, William Laverick from Sunderland, had "three on left hand for throwing ink in absence of teacher", and in April 1940, J Telfer had "three on left hand for rough play with skipping rope in playground".

Once aged eleven, children attended Swavesey School, as did Jean Walker who lived in Swavesey in a cottage without running water. Like other children, she was very jealous because "settlement" children were given "Vulcan" bikes, and she and others would shout, "Go on home you old miners". Bob Carter's son Bobby would yell back, "We're not old miners". He told me although the locals were antagonistic "we northerners were a tougher bunch", and described how he tormented Jean. She liked to keep all her pens and pencils tidy in a box, but he would borrow them and muddle them up and tip them all over her desk. Sitting behind her he used to pull her hair. Infuriated, Jean would put up her hand to complain, "Please Miss, Bobby Carter's pulling my hair". Not a good beginning for a romance you might think!

The villagers experienced a big change in their landscape as can be seen from its description in May 1943 in "A Record of 8 Years Progress".

"The Estate was purchased in 1935 ... previous to that date it had been run for many years as a corn farm and the land was in very poor heart. Very little farmyard manure had been used and the only livestock were a few pigs, a cow and about six horses. The corn crops were light on most parts of the estate and one piece of land planted with potatoes in 1935 lifted about 2 tons to the acre, the tubers being only seed size. ...At that time there were about 220 acres of arable land in fields of from 20 – 50 acres and 120 acres of pasture (including 76 acres of fen land which flooded at certain times of the year). 40 acres of the pasture were later sold".

In under two years, stretching out from the village into the south-west quarter of the parish, a smallholding estate was established. On each holding were the houses of red brick outnumbering the traditional village properties. There were glasshouses, piggeries with up to 40 pigs, poultry sheds and about 100 to 150 hens and some goats and horses.

The first of the cottages were of red brick, plain, with gable ends and were

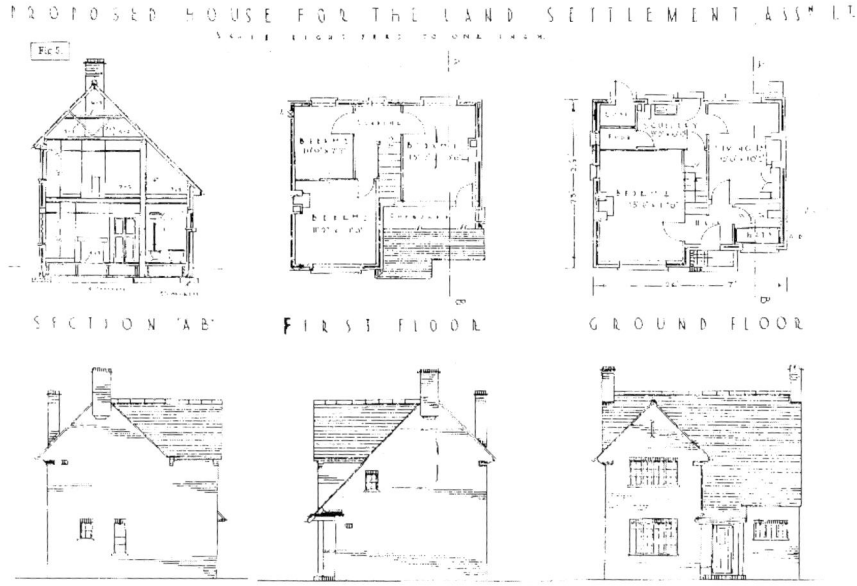

PROPOSED HOUSE FOR THE LAND SETTLEMENT ASS" LT

SECTION 'A B'   FIRST FLOOR   GROUND FLOOR

Fred C. Levitt of Biggleswade designed the houses numbered between 27 and 37 Cootes Lane. He designed similar houses for the LSA's Estates at Chawston, Wyboston and Potton in Bedfordshire, and also glasshouses for the LSA.

semi-detached. They were built by Pannett and Needen, a London firm. Mr L.G. Thorpe, builder, of Over, lent his carpenter and Arthur Burling, a sixteen year old apprentice, to help build them. By the time the second phase of housing was begun, the Association had appointed its own architects, including Fred C. Levitt, of Biggleswade. He designed varied detached houses for Cootes Lane. They were similar to those he designed for Chawston and Wyboston Estates in Bedfordshire.

In the 1st Annual Report, 1936, of the Land Settlement Association, the vice-chairman of the LSA stated,

"In designing the cottages a further object has been to ensure that the old gibe of 'Queen Anne in front and Mary Anne at the back' shall have no force. Front back and sides have decent comely faces...."

Fred Levitt's Cootes Lane houses were varied in design and, like the other Estate houses, were far superior to those of many local people.
They had a downstairs bathroom, and a "Triplex" fire grate with a cooking oven, and a back boiler for heating the hot water system. No wonder poorer villagers were envious for they used earth closets and fetched water from the village pump.

Villagers, like the Ingle family of the High Street living in a dilapidated home, envied the settlers their plots of land and new houses with superior facilities. Perhaps they would not have minded that the lavatories of some of the Cootes Lane houses were inconvenient because they had to be entered from outdoors. Jack Jobling's daughter-in-law, Sadie, explained that on windy nights the whole household would be woken when the door crashed behind anyone who wanted "to go". But at least they flushed. The locals would not have envied the facilities chosen by a different estate's pompous Local Advisory Committee. It decided that a non-flushing lavatory in a shed would be good enough for "that class" of house.

Apart from the enticements of friendly social activities (to be described later), the villagers benefited from the newcomers' presence in other ways.

34

They acquired an improved bus service because the incomers wished to visit St Ives for entertainment or to shop, or visit the doctor. It was reported in the "Cambridge Weekly News" that on 23 April 1937, Traffic Commissioners for the Eastern Area heard applications from rival bus companies who wished to provide the more appropriately timed services that had been requested by the Land Settlement tenants. Barker's bus Services Ltd, offered the most suitable timetable.

More importantly, the villagers gained jobs from the LSA and were employed for a variety of tasks at the Central Farm, and local farmers were contracted by the Association for such tasks as ploughing and combine-harvesting.

Nevertheless, there were those who did not welcome the "outgoing" northerners. One villager told me she had thought the newcomers were "a race apart", and seemed "cocky". Many of the closely related villagers were far more reserved than the newcomers, and some were as cantankerous as those that had driven the curates to leave the village in earlier times. Virgy's grandmother Giddings, who was religious, did not hide her disapproval of settlers' wives who visited the pub on Sundays. And for a long time the newcomers were not accepted onto the Parish Council even though one councillor resigned because he was so disgusted by his fellow councillors' attitude.

Returned North

The school register shows that for many who arrived with high hopes, the dream of a new life ended almost before it began. "Returned N.", the teacher wrote by numerous of the new entrants' names after only a few months or even only weeks. By some she added, "returned from the North", so perhaps they had just been visiting relatives. For various reasons there was constant change during the first four years as families arrived or left.

The would be settlers found it difficult to embrace a completely alien rural way of life in the very flat landscape, hundreds of miles away from their families and friends, amongst people who spoke differently. They were homesick. The miners missed the Associations and Institutes and Miners' Clubs which were sources of entertainment, camaraderie, friendship and also, romance. For example, Ron Foster remembered a Gala, a political gathering of miners from different collieries which was held annually in

35

Durham City, when miners marched with their colliery banners held high, waving to the crowds and singing at the top of their voices. They "let down their hair and had a good time and drank a few beers", said Ron. His father, Tim, met Florence, Ron's mother, at a Gala, and married her the very next Gala day.

A trip to the seaside at Hunstanton c1937. It was the first outing arranged for Fen Drayton's new settlers by the LSA. Edward Stott has photographed his family and that of Tim Foster from Page Bank who is standing at the back.
I to r: Ronald, Tim junior and George Foster. Tim's wife, Florence, is holding Edward's baby, while Edward's three other children pose next to Mrs Stott. The newly arrived families appear apprehensive about the strange new world they have entered but they are simply unused to being photographed. Nevertheless, the Stott family eventually returned to Sunderland.

There were no leek growing clubs or whippet and pigeon racing in the south and the food was different. Dishes the northerners would have enjoyed were described to me by a settler's daughter-in-law (more of her later), who tasted them when she visited Sunderland. New to her were pie and peas, Leek pie, baked herrings, Peas Pudding, and a split bun containing chitterlings. She said the northern ice cream made by Italians, including the Notrianni family, was far nicer than that sold at home.

A New Life

Daily tasks could be lonely and tedious on the holdings, especially for men used to working alongside others and for their wives used to popping in and out of the homes of their friends and families in neighbourhoods where several generations lived in close proximity. The men disliked the humdrum planting procedures and being tied to the holdings and crops that needed watering morning and evening. It is said that ex-miners in particular hated working outside in all weathers. In any case it was hard for them to make a living, even the most conscientious that worked long tiring hours. Bob Carter, for one, received the dole for two to three years because he was not making enough money to live on.

Tommy Collier (son of "Tot") remembered transporting produce to a depot in Bateman Street, Cambridge, and said that flowers, tomatoes and fruit were transported to Liverpool, Birmingham and Coventry via Swavesey Station, and to London, but the produce was often returned unsold to be dumped up by Spring Hill. Lettuce prices could be affected by cold weather but the men still had to pay charges whatever they got for their produce. Although the families didn't have much money at least they ate well.

The level of men's incomes was also affected by the prevalence of pests and diseases such as swine fever, potato blight, club root in brassicas, and fowl pest. In 1938 there was a devastating poultry epidemic on several LSA estates including Fen Drayton, causing Kit Messenger for one, to abandon poultry keeping. He hadn't the heart to start again. Chickens and pigs were usually the settlers' bread and butter. They could always sell eggs, some through Hunts Egg and Poultry Packers Ltd. These kept them going during the winter lull. Although Tot Collier hated the area and missed working with the pit horses, he made the best of it. Bob Carter, however, loved his life on the land. Rhubarb growing was a speciality of his and he like others managed to survive by using other strategies.

The rules forbade paid work away from the holdings, nevertheless, some settlers supplemented their earnings by hedging and ditching for Keith Wright, a local farmer. The warden turned a blind eye as the men badly needed the money. They also broke another of the rules of the Tenancy Agreement. Despite being forbidden, the selling of produce privately seems to have been commonplace although those caught in illicit selling could be thrown off their holdings. Bobby Carter explained how his father would pay the local tradesmen in kind, and sold produce in the pub and to local shops. One settler was thrown off the estate early on for the rather more serious offence of stealing glass.

A number of settlers and wives were unfit. Some miners had lung problems as did Tot Collier whose chest could be heard wheezing, but he struggled on while others gave up their holdings because of ill health. Failed LSA settlers were allowed to live in Fen Drayton House, to give them time to make new plans, after they chose to leave or were dismissed from the scheme. The Unemployment Assistance Board bore the expense of their removal from the Estate back to their home areas or to another part of the country. Quite a number of failed settlers stayed in the area. Tommy Lumley, a former miner, at first returned to Esh Winning after leaving his Mill Road holding, but returned again to Fen Drayton when the mine was closed down because there were better prospects of employment. Walter Messenger, former miner at the Waterhouses Colliery, also gave up his holding. A widower, he found he could not earn enough on his holding to raise his four daughters. He discovered he could earn more at Keith Wright's Dairy at nearby Fenstanton, as did other failed settlers. He lived for quite a while in Fen Drayton House until The Orchard council houses were built.

Because of the mixed abilities of those attempting the new life, it was unsurprising that many gave up the struggle for it was a difficult time for anyone involved in horticultural and agricultural production.

"In his book "East Anglia, 1939", R. Douglas-Brown wrote "nearly 1,300,000 workers had left the land between 1931 and the later months of 1938. ... At a long series of meetings, farmers' voices were heard running through the gamut of anxiety, frustration, despair and anger".

Rare Old Do's

Those that embraced the new way of life did their best to compensate for the missing camaraderie enjoyed in their former lives. Next to the village school, in the heart of the village, the presence of the northerners in the once quiet Three Tuns, made it a magnet for people from many villages, including Bluntisham, Earith, Swavesey, Over, Fenstanton, Hilton and St Ives. Joe and Martha Green, the publicans, benefited and took on more help. "Pa" and Ma", as the northerners called them, had strict rules, and only Tot Collier was allowed to play their precious piano. Ladies could not go into the bar and were only allowed into the parlour at weekends. Darts and dominoes were played and lovely singsongs participated in said Bobby Carter. The pub-goers performed their favourites. Tot Collier (an ex army man) would sing "Trumpeter, what are you sounding there?" Bob Carter's speciality was "One alone to be my own", from the "Desert Song",

Bob and Ellen Rose Carter with children Bobby, Rose and Barbara. They are contented with their new life on the Springhill Road holding far away from the Sunderland shipbuilding and mining area they had left, where the scourge of unemployment had caused the failure of their businesses.

learned from the theatrical lodgers back home. Bobby Carter (when in his eighties) gave me a rendition of a ditty of "Weller" Burton's, (he was the brother of Tom Burton who kept a pet hen). Weller, a likeable villager if a bit simple, would sing "Martha Green loves me, I love her too. We blush when we meet, like true lovers do". Everyone had a good time. The pub was an important part of their lives. Tim Foster, used to the sociability of the miners' clubs after a day spent down the mine, would be found nearly every evening in the bar just drinking and chatting or maybe playing a game of dominoes, said his son. Evidently not even floods would stop him: undaunted he would arrive for his usual tipple via a detour of three miles. To those who had drunk too much Martha, considered a rude woman by some and feared by local children, would say "get you home you've had enough". She would especially target men who had several children and she knew couldn't afford to drink.

On one occasion the settlers went on a pub crawl around the villages. At a Cottenham hostelry they were joined by the Salvation Army and revelled in the singing of "Onward Christian Soldiers" and other hymns. A villager told me the men were so popular they were enticed to return again with the promise of free beer. Can this be true?

Because the LSA wished to foster a sense of community when bringing so many strangers together on its estates, it leased out land at a peppercorn rent at Fen Drayton, and the National Council of Social Services contributed to a Village Hall built on it in September 1938. Situated close to the Central Services Area at Middleton Farm, it became a focal point for the whole village. At weekends, after ten o'clock in the evening, men would move there from the pub for further entertainment.

Dances and entertainment of many kinds were held in the new hall, including that provided by various small bands. Twenty men could play mouth organs, and there was one fiddle and one drum. Locals, including Mr Ingle, joined in. On these occasions Mr Carter acted as MC. "They were lovely concerts, rare old do's said Bobby Carter. Mr Cassidy, a settler, played the violin and his daughter ballet danced. Tim Foster would play the "squeeze box" - accordion. Huge trays of slab cake (iced sponge cake) made by Mrs Carter were cut into squares for refreshments. Bob Carter was nice but firm, he was the one to intervene to stop fights instigated by a particular trouble-maker and his cronies. I was told that the trouble-makers came mostly from St Ives. I have to believe it. In December of 1938, the Village Hall Committee arranged a party treat for 150 children,

Getting into the swing of things. Jack and Rosemary Jobling tend the outdoor tomato crop on their holding in Cootes Lane. They had worked hard to produce the crop but thought it infinitely preferable to Jack's previous life when he had spent so many hours searching unsuccessfully for work in the shipyards and mines.

and a carnival was held in the hall on Boxing Day where Walter Messenger, dressed as a Viennese Officer, was awarded a prize. The provision of a hall, and the influx of newcomers, led to the formation of Fen Drayton's branch of the Women's Institute in 1938.

Life on the estate

In 1988 "Babs" Burns described to me her experience as a late arrival from a Special Area. She said her husband John, an unemployed chef, took a job in South Shields, "propping", that is, unloading boats of pit props from such countries as Norway and Poland. Low pay and poor, cramped, living conditions, led John to leave for Fen Drayton in April 1939, where his brother-in-law, Mr Brownson, was a trainee settler. John's wife and little girl joined him on a rainy 5th November at 39 Middleton Way. The house seemed huge and empty. It had no floor covering and only a few items of furniture and was without electricity until the following day. Babs was struck by the quiet, such a contrast to town life. Mrs Bennet and Mrs Thorndyke visited her. They were Welfare visitors who provided blankets, clothes and shoes where needed.

Two years had passed before John Burns began to repay the LSA a loan of £500. Babs said it was a hard life for women. Besides working on the holdings for long hours with their children alongside in prams, they had also the household chores to do. She considered the women worked harder than the men and said some families would have been better off if the men hadn't spent so much time in the pub.

Mrs Burns described herself and her husband as townies who "didn't know a weed from a blade of grass". This was to have unfortunate consequences. One morning her husband asked her to clear, that is weed, the carrot bed. After she had been weeding for quite some time the warden, Mr Piper, arrived and gave her unwelcome information. He told her she had pulled out the carrots and left in the weeds. Her husband was not at all pleased but she herself thought it very funny. Winters, she said, were particularly difficult and she and her husband relied on their two pig-sties to keep them going when there wasn't anything else. She explained how they made tomato cloches from Dutch lights wired together to form a ridge and set them on top of bales of straw to add height and how, with other settlers,

In 1939, on their holding in Springhill Road, Ellen Rose Carter takes a break from the chores to enjoy a frivolous moment with her children. Rose, aged five, enjoys a ride on Betsy pig, who was a very good mother with a soft nature, whilst Barbara is supervising.

they trundled their produce in two-wheeled barrows down to the black shed before there was a packing station.

Fred Kitchen, an Oxcroft Estate tenant between 1945 and 1947, wrote in "Settlers on the land" that: *"The settlers gained expert advice, technical advisers, freedom of worry from bookkeeping, and obtaining plants and chicks but needed their health, strength and a large family"*.
He said the men had some independence but:

"Very definitely the Land Settlement was not founded as a Home for the Sick, Lame, or Lazy".

Although the Land Settlement experiment was a godsend for some, the prospect of fresh food, comfortable homes and better health did not attract sufficient new applicants to the scheme. The Special Areas category was extended in 1938 to include men from South Wales. As a consequence three Welsh families, two from Trealaw in the Rhonda valley and another from Nantyglo, Bryn Mawr, settled at Fen Drayton in 1939. By then, training was undertaken on designated estates, so Tom Pope, Jack George, and William Williams had already completed theirs before arriving.

Welsh miners, Jack George & Tom Pope, third and fourth from the left on the back row, at a designated training centre at Siddlesham estate. Here they spent 12 weeks in 1939 getting physically fit and gaining some elementary knowledge of pigs, poultry keeping and cultivations under glass.

On their Middleton Way holdings, horse ploughing was not practicable on the difficult heavy clay clods. To solve the problem a cultivator and a plough, powered by two steam engines, were brought in.

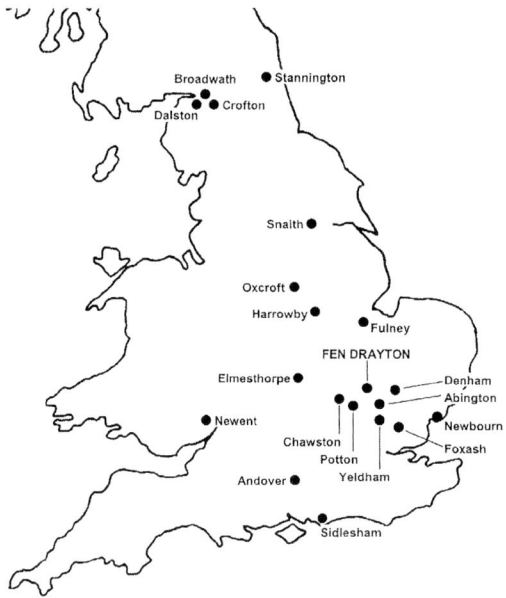

The LSA's full-time small holding estates developed by 1935

The booklet, "The Healthy Future", was published c1938. In it the LSA advertised itself as "an organisation that provided capital and knowledge for those who had ambitions to go on the land but would normally be unable to do so". The LSA made some holdings available to unemployed men outside the designated Special Areas. 16 holdings at Rookery Farm, Wyboston, part of the Chawston Estate in Bedfordshire, were reserved for the London unemployed. They were partly funded by the City Parochial Charities and the Carnegie United Kingdom Trust.

Theta's Lovely Life

Theta, Kit Messenger's daughter (she who was smacked at school) said it was a lovely life for children on the holdings even though they had to help on the land from a very early age. She enjoyed helping with the chickens and pigs and having a pony and would prick out tomato seedlings for pocket money with her friend Beryl Williams. Bobby Carter, too, enjoyed the life, although he had to feed the chickens and also hand milk the goats before he went to school and again when he came home. At the age of 12 years he had to help when a farrowing sow was having difficulties. He had to lie by her and be aware of when she "pained" and help the piglet into the world. Bobby remembered Wessex and Large White were the Associations pedigree herds. His father was awarded a prize for a Large White Gilt after he had washed, powdered and manicured it for a competition.

Bill Laverick with son Billy. Children loved riding their ponies around Fen Drayton.

Theta said, that in winter the children had fun floating in baths on flooded fields, or revelled in skating when the water froze, and that in summer they enjoyed picnics by the river with other families. She said she felt like part of one big happy family. The families were visited by relatives including Bobby's uncle Tom, an out of work miner suffering from silicosis, a lung disease. Anne Laverick's great-granddad came down from Sunderland to help with the pea picking whilst enjoying a holiday at the same time. Anne was only thirteen when she arrived in 1939, but did not attend school because her father decided she should work on the holding instead. Luckily she liked the work.

After leaving school at fourteen Bobby, as did Theta and other youngsters, bred rabbits to earn money. He would sell their fur to the furrier in Bridge Street, St Ives and the carcasses to Len Anderson the butcher just across the road from the furrier. A Chinchilla pelt was more valuable than the meat. A good silver one was worth 1/6d. He kept 20 to 30 rabbits whose number could increase to 200 with the arrival of their babies. He received less money for the wild rabbits he snared.

To gain local sympathy and support a Local Advisory Committee was appointed for each estate. It was drawn from prominent persons in the district such as landowners and representatives of local authorities. Mr W. S. Mansfield was the first Chairman of Fen Drayton's Advisory Committee, which included Captain Fred Johnson of the local farming family, Mr Unwin of Unwin's Seeds and Miss Chivers of the Chivers jam and fruit canning family.

Miss Chivers took some of the settlement children under her wing. She befriended Bobby Carter, Les Cassidy, Johnny Jobling, George Finley (known as Cranston), and Matthew (Mattie) Scott. Bobby said she bought his first pair of long trousers when he was 14 years old. She would also take the children for rides in her Bullnose Morris car around the villages, and to the Chivers factory at Histon where she gave them items such as jams and jellies to take home. She would also take products from the factory to Fen Drayton Village Hall to be distributed among settler families.

The LSA Managers

Regional Administrators who were each responsible for six or seven estates
would advise the Estate Wardens. The Wardens managed individual
estates and on them such staff as an accountant, a pig man, a poultry man,
a packing shed manager and lorry and tractor drivers.

In 1974, K. J. McCready summed up the value of the Wardens (by then
known as Managers). He wrote:

*"The Estate Managers are also the people who have the greatest individual effect
on the success or failure of their estates and hence on the Association as a whole".*

Philip Hamlett, who we will meet again, had a long career with the LSA
from 1946 to 1985, and then worked for a further period until 1991 because
of closure problems. He began work with the LSA as a tractor driver then,
after being in charge of cultivations and farming and pigs at Andover
Estate, became personal assistant to the Southern Regional Administrator
for three years.

He managed several of the seven estates on which he worked including
Abington and Fen Drayton in
Cambridgeshire and rose to become a
senior manager. Dr Peter Clarke, an
Economist, described him to me as the
best. He endeavoured to give applicants
a realistic assessment of their chance
of success on a holding, and he was
kindly, conscientious and caring, helping
tenants who went to him with personal
problems.

Over the years Fen Drayton managers,
of which there were at least ten, would
have varying strengths and weaknesses.
For example, it seems that Mr Thompson
was an innovator improving on Mr
Piper's good record while one manager,
though well liked by the men, was
too soft-hearted and resisted change.
Another, I was told, was not up to

Mr Piper the first warden at Fen Drayton

48

the task when times became especially difficult and he had a depressing effect on an estate. Mr Tom Scott, however, manager from 1953–1967, was another who was spoken of highly. He had many of the necessary qualities.

Tom was a former Pig Technical Assistant who Roger Robinson, a former tenant, described as a "fantastic manager" who "had time if you needed him". Roger, from a farming background, said Tom's horticultural expertise was of great help to him when he was a beginner. Roger's neighbour Derek Robinson (no relation), Mrs Cox and Alan Hunter of Cootes Lane were among those who thought Tom was an excellent manager. Several tenants thought he was strict, some said bad tempered but that he had a soft side. He would mix with the men and help anyone in need and arrange assistance for anyone who was sick. Derek Tuck, the former Farm and Transport Manager explained, as did several growers,

1957 - Tom Scott , the manager of the estate, showing new tenants Alan & Doreen Hunter, the holding at No. 14 Cootes Lane. Here they began their lives as smallholders

that Tom preferred to help those who were conscientious. It was said that he would advise men on the best crops to grow on a particular patch of soil and was a good judge of what would grow well. Importantly, Derek Robinson explained, he kept men's finances in order whereas some managers would allow men to take on debts they couldn't manage. To introduce the smallholders to up-to-date ideas he took them on visits to different estates and experimental stations. He was capable when negotiating with Marks and Spencer to obtain orders and was also a very good cricket player who played for St Ives and he encouraged community spirit on the estate.

Despite all the help and advice given them the tenants' productivity varied enormously. It was said that those who were keen, intelligent, hard working and planned their work properly, were successful and made three times the profit of the less competent. But even so they struggled against circumstances beyond their control.

To begin with the location of their estate could increase the men's chances of success or failure. For instance, Oxcroft Estate near Chesterfield in Derbyshire was situated on exposed tableland and suffered heavy atmospheric pollution and poor light intensity. It was also subject to subsidence because of old mine workings. Stannington in Northumberland also suffered from cold exposed conditions. While settlers on the warmer Siddlesham Estate, situated on the south coast, incurred lower heating costs, and also benefited from good light intensity, which helped them achieve higher production levels than those of the more northerly estates.

Eight to ten acre holdings on poorer land, like those at Abington, were biased towards pig and poultry keeping, with some horticulture. The holdings of between three and six acres on better soil, such as those at Fen Drayton and Potton, were biased towards horticulture with some pigs and poultry. The Association promoted the concept "that diversity on the holdings provides security", the "three legged stool" of horticulture, pigs and poultry. But Stannington's 12 acre holdings were completely devoted to livestock and uniquely, Fulney Estate in Lincolnshire (close to Spalding renowned for its annual Tulip Festival), was a 100% horticultural estate. Its holdings of two to four acres on silt rich land were used for forced bulb production until the late 1960s.

Daffodil bulbs on at least one occasion were transferred from Fulney to a field on the Harrowby Estate in Yorkshire and returned to Fulney Estate later. One year, Philip Hamlett planted some remnants at Abington but disappointingly they failed to flower. He learned later that they had suffered heart rot. That news would have been a bitter blow to Fulney's tenants.

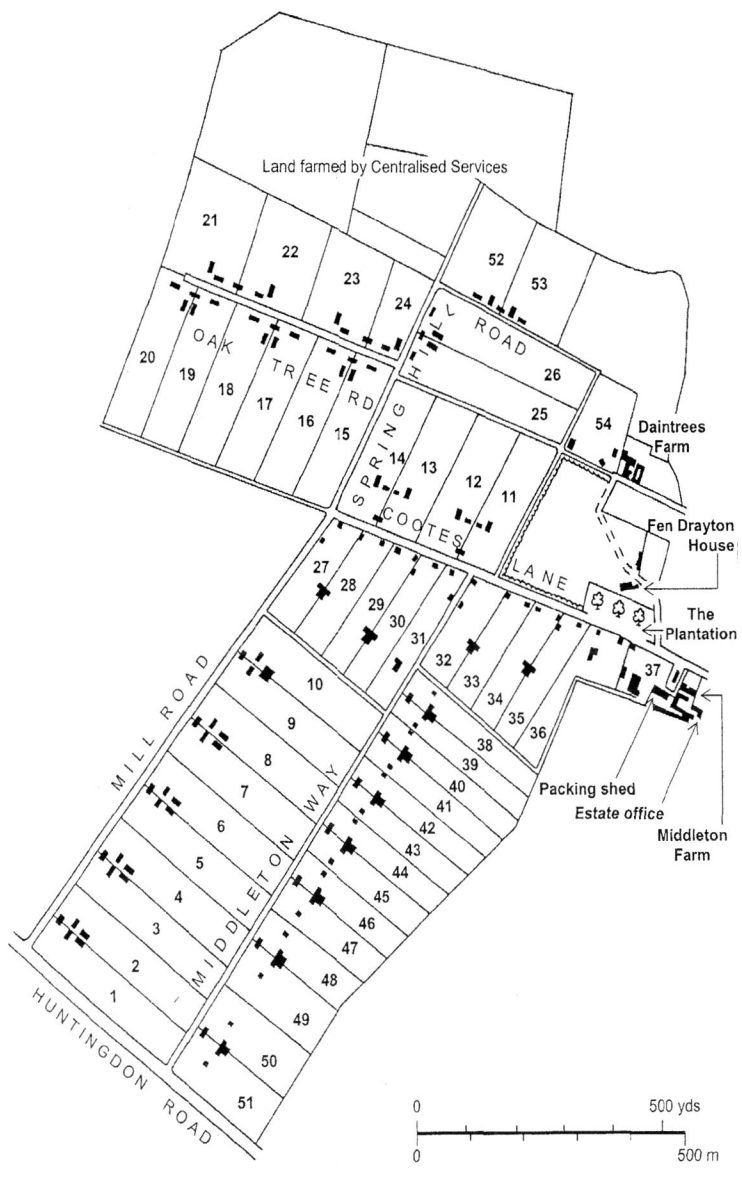

Map of Fen Drayton's Smallholding Estate

By 1939 twenty estates had been developed with no plans for more because it was considered that the costly scheme had had limited success. However, the nation would soon have cause to be thankful that the estates had been created. On 3 September 1939 people huddled around their wireless sets heard the Prime Minister, Neville Chamberlain, announce ominous news to the nation from the Cabinet Room at Westminster. He said "This country is at war with Germany". World War II had begun.

Chapter 3
1939 – 1945 A New Purpose

At the outbreak of war there were twenty LSA smallholding estates occupying a total of 9,817 acres of land. On them were 1,000 smallholdings with an efficient structure to support the 800 families who were endeavouring to escape from a life of unemployment. The threat to Britain's survival solved the problem of industrial unemployment but created another, the threat of disruption to the country's food supplies. The LSA was ready and willing to take up a new challenge. While continuing to support and advise the settlers and their families from the Special Areas, the Association would use the estates to support the war effort. They would help to feed the nation.

To help the estates produce the maximum amount of food in the shortest possible time the Association changed its outlook and structure. It discontinued recruiting from the Special Areas and disbanded the training schemes. From this time applicants would need agricultural experience and also some capital of their own. They would be described as "Agricultural Tenants".

c1940, Cyril Hayler, one of the first Agricultural Tenants at Fen Drayton, is with son Richard at 33 Cootes Lane. Middleton Way's smallholdings are in view.

53

By 1941 about one quarter of the LSA's tenants were of this new category and came from wide ranging agricultural backgrounds. One of them was Cyril Hayler who had held a responsible position at a market garden. He took the tenancy of 33 Cootes Lane in 1940. As an incoming tenant he had to pay the outgoing settler for equipment and all growing crops on the holding. Manured ground also had a value. Although he provided £500 to become an Agricultural Tenant, he was governed by the same rules as settlers from the Special Areas. At least one person of this new type of tenant was anxious to emphasise to me that he had been an Agricultural Tenant. It seemed he felt a cut above the original settlers.

The Estates' central farms ploughed and cultivated any spare land, and settlers were encouraged to concentrate on what they grew best, but some were called away to priority jobs or into the fighting forces. William Laverick and Bob Carter were directed back to the shipyards. When Bob left to be a Plater at Doxfords, the Tyneside shipbuilders, his wife Ellen Rose, moved from 25 to 52 Springhill Road, which had no land. In contrast, Rosemary Jobling chose to continue on Jack's holding whilst he was in the R.A.F. Alice Messenger also managed Kit's holding in Middleton Way whilst he was based at Lord's Bridge Bomb Storage Depot in Cambridgeshire.

A very new arrival, Doris Scutt, sister-in-law of Cyril Hayler, also took on the challenge of cultivating the holding when her husband Jim was conscripted to the R.A.F. in 1941. Newly married they were separated only eleven days after their wedding and ten days after receiving the key to 31 Cootes Lane. Jim was conscripted despite an LSA official's reassurance that he would be exempt from call-up. Their new home, vacated by evacuees, had been left in such a disgusting state it needed fumigating, and for some time Doris was pestered about debts the evacuees had left unpaid, including those to Robert Sayles of Cambridge. Doris had another problem to contend with during her first winter for bucketfuls of snow had to be removed from the loft. It was discovered that no felt had been laid under the roof tiles.

In 1941, Doris Scutt is strawberry picking whilst on a visit to her sister Muriel Hayler at No. 33 Cootes Lane. Doris and her husband Jim settled at No. 31 that year but almost immediately, as we shall see, they received a rude awakening.

Rosemary Jobling and Doris Scutt managed successfully with the help of the Women's Land Army girls like Elsie Corn, Mona Dorritt and Win Blackburn who lived in, and later with that of Italian, Austrian and German Prisoners of War, of whom some were only 17 years of age when they arrived from the camp at Elsworth. Each morning the teenaged Theta Messenger would cycle ahead of the prisoners to guide them to their allocated holdings where, ironically, the POW's were helping the smallholders grow food which would help Britain to survive, including that supplied to the NAAFI's at the airfields.

At Fen Drayton it was impossible to forget there was a war on. Besides the evacuees taken into the homes of villagers and settlers, there was a Home Guard unit in which both communities were represented and, because of the fear of imminent invasion, an army check point, based at two houses in Middleton Way. But predominantly it was the noise and the tremendous activity overhead in the skies that they could not escape. Thousands of planes passed over the estate each day (one million passed over Cambridgeshire in 1944). Observers would count them as they left and when they returned bedraggled and separated. Jim Scutt, whilst home

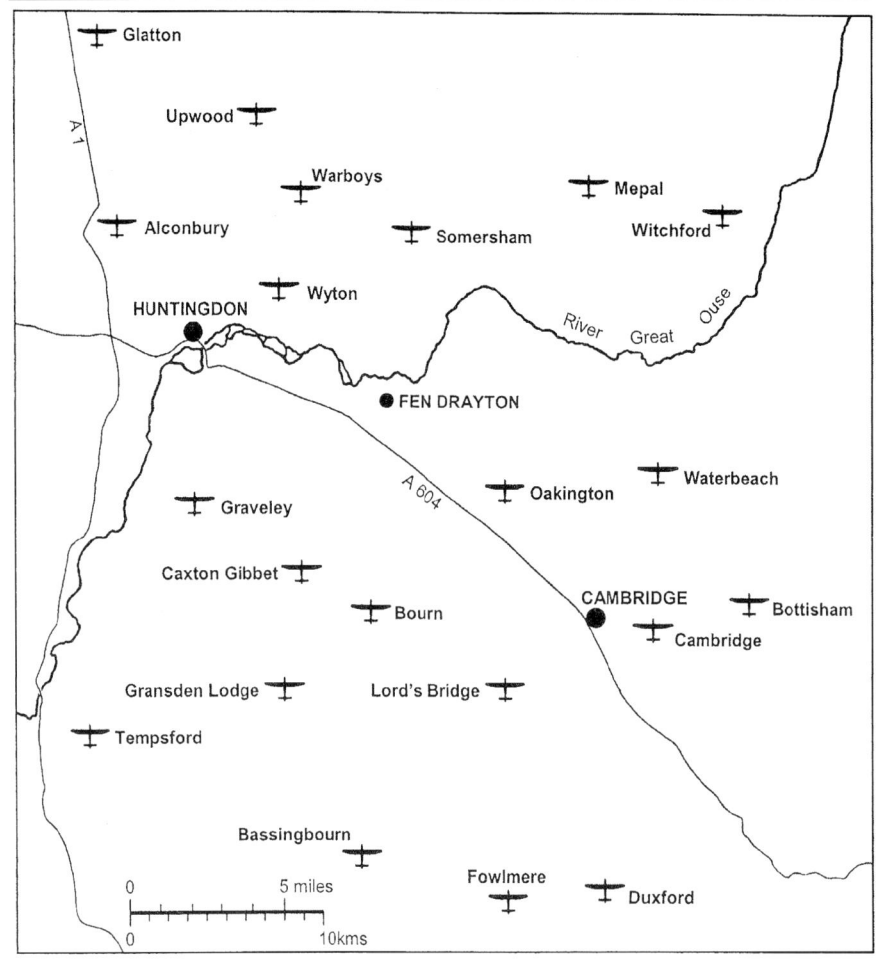

World War II airfields in Cambridgeshire.
Planes of R.A.F. Bomber Command and the Eighth Air Force set out from Cambridgeshire to bomb targets all over Europe, and every day thousands of planes flew over Fen Drayton. The American bombers went out on daylight raids while the R.A.F. flew at night.
Produce grown by Fen Drayton's smallholders was supplied to a number of these airfields as well as to others outside Cambridgeshire.

on leave, watched with apprehension as a B17 Flying Fortress limped back to base over the estate. Its tail end had been damaged and pieces were hanging loose. At other times he saw and heard hundreds of planes gathering in the surrounding skies to get into formation before setting out to bomb strategic enemy positions. Villagers and smallholders spoke of other occasions when they saw great numbers of gliders being towed above them, at times taking part in exercises in preparation for "D Day" on the 6 June, 1944, and then again to be included in the armadas of gliders which would be towed from eastern airfields during 16 - 18 September for the massive airborne landing attempt at Arnhem, Holland. They provided a spectacular sight. Ron Foster, as a school boy, saw that it took a whole day for the planes to pass over in wave after wave.

A B17F 'Hell's Angels' of the 303rd Bomb Group photographed at Molesworth on 10 October 1943. This one must have flown over Fen Drayton many times, explained Michael Bowyer, an Aviation Historian. Perhaps it was the one Jim Scutt watched, with much trepidation, when it limped over Fen Drayton with its tail badly damaged.

Because of the new markets created by the war, the settlers' incomes began to improve. Fen Drayton's Estate produced huge amounts of food for the air bases by which it was surrounded. Bassingbourn, Kettering, Oakington, Upwood, Waterbeach and Wyton (home to the legendary Pathfinder Force), among other airfields, received deliveries sometimes twice a day. Theta Messenger, by now an LSA employee, described how she plucked chickens for the NAAFI headquarters at Caxton, which also received lorry loads of cabbages, soft fruits, potatoes, root vegetables and cut flowers from the Estate. Mr Ward, the deputy warden at that time, told me that it was a very enjoyable time in many ways although he worked a seven-day week. Once, after arriving home late and tired after a hard day's work, he was instructed to prepare twenty tons of potatoes immediately for a contingent of American airmen. They had just arrived after crossing the Atlantic in the liner Queen Mary.

Mrs Burns, the townie, who hadn't known a carrot from a weed, said there were no days off. There were never enough hours and with double summer time they all often worked until midnight. It seemed as though they hardly went to bed. In fact, she said, literally some nights they did not go to bed. Doris Scutt said she would rise for a 4 a.m. start. The smallholders as usual had to contend with wind and frost damage, glass houses that shattered easily, and visitations of pests such as cabbage fly, carrot fly, pea weevil and wire worm. Some, like Tim Foster from Pagebank, concentrated on growing vegetables and stopped keeping chickens and goats, but others continued with pigs, feeding them on kitchen waste collected from the R.A.F. bases (with the occasional tea spoon thrown in). Pig and poultry numbers on other LSA estates were much reduced as animal feed became scarce.

Between 1941 and 1944 life was unsettled for the Head of Fen Drayton School too. Once again class sizes were fluctuating. Not only tenants' children, but also evacuees from the bombing, came and went. Some came from the north to stay with relatives on the holdings but the majority were from London and Essex who were given homes by smallholders and villagers alike. Between 3 June 1940 and 3 December 1940, 77 evacuee children arrived, including 24 admitted on one day, and another 40 on 2 October. There were numerous arrivals until September 1944.

At Easter in April 1940, Mr Rufus H Mallinson, the headmaster, who had only arrived in the previous October, sent a report to all the parents describing the poor situation at the school but, most interestingly, he compared the abilities and shortcomings of the three groups of children. Virginia Giddings' grandparents, with whom she lived, received a copy (Charlie Giddings was Horse Keeper, first for Mr Evison and then for the LSA). What they thought of Mr Mallinson's comments she doesn't remember. But he described the children as follows:

"Fen Drayton Natives Well-behaved and quiet. Not intelligent but comparatively industrious, and nearly up to average in their School work.

Land Settlement children. An entirely different class in many ways. Many are highly intelligent, but they are lazy and entirely without ambition. Their School work is very bad indeed, and it is astonishing to me to see such intelligent looking children so extremely poor at their work. I do not think that a single L.S. scholar at this School is anywhere near the average mark. They are vociferous and noisy, but none the worse for that, and they are on the whole well-behaved, though they show themselves clever only in dodging school work. Many of these children have never done an honest day's work in their lives. Their attendance at School is very bad indeed, and I fully expect that many of their parents will find themselves in trouble on this matter next term. Little or no interest shown by parents."

But at least they were superior to the evacuees.

"Evacuees. … Not nearly so intelligent as the L.S. children, but, like them, without any ambition to work. Their discipline is generally bad, and they make for most of the difficulty in running this School. Their book work is especially wretched, and they appear to be quite happy in their miserable school condition. But their attendance at School is splendid, and an example to both of the above Sections".

It seems that in spite of the headmaster's best efforts things did not improve. In February 1945, because of parents' complaints, Mr Piper the Warden wrote to the Association about the bad arrangements at the school. He explained that the standard of education was very poor with teachers being changed at six weekly intervals. One "normal" boy was said to be still unable to read or write although 12 years old. Mr Piper was very concerned that he would be unable to recruit the right type of tenant if conditions did not improve. Letters were hastily written between the powers that be in the LSA and Cambridgeshire Education Committee was persuaded to allow a schoolmaster to continue after his allotted six weeks. It was reported that he had had a positive effect on learning and discipline.

Fen Drayton School 1940. Miss Sherwood and Mrs Bradshaw an evacuee teacher who lived with the Messengers. The evacuees were taught in the Village Hall until Easter when they were incorporated into the village school. Mr M. K. Kidd was acting Head at that time.

The headmaster said of the northern children, "They are vociferous and noisy, but none the worse for that, and they are on the whole well-behaved, though they show themselves clever only in dodging school work". See appendix for names.

General Report and Open Letter to Parents

Easter 1941

Scholar's Name. *Virginia Stebbings*   Age   6

No. of times absent from school since the beginning of the
School Year, September 19th last:-

                                              times absent.

GENERAL REPORT

This is the first report I have been able to send to
Parents since my coming here last October. It has taken me
a long time to know very much about the School in its present
difficult circumstances, and my report must still be a general
one, though I shall forward a detailed one at end the of the
Summer Term.

This School has apparently been through some difficult
times, and the work is below the average. When I came here
there was no kind of discipline in the Senior Section of the
School, and where there is no discipline there cannot be any
work proceeding. A School is usually judged by the condition
of its Senior Class, and the Senior Class at Fen Drayton is
in an almost hopeless condition, much worse than either of the
other two sections. One cause of this backwardness among the
older children is their shocking attendance at school, and some-
thing is undoubtedly else where. Another is the lack of
interest shown by parents, and this, I think, must be one of
the real causes of these children's backwardness.

There are three entirely different classes of children
attending this School, and it is interesting to see them all
in one school. A brief report on these three sets of children
would run like this:-

Fen Drayton Natives. Well-behaved and quiet. Not intelligent
but comparatively industrious, and nearly up to average in
their School work. Attendance at School reasonably good.
Land Settlement Children. An entirely different class in
many ways. Many are highly intelligent, but they are lazy
and entirely without ambition. Their School work is very
bad indeed, and it is astonishing to me to see such intelligent
looking children so extremely poor at their work. I do not
think that a single L.S. scholar at this School is anywhere
near the average mark. They are vociferous and noisy, but
none the worse for that, and they are on the whole well-
behaved, though they show themselves clever only in dodging
School work. Many of these children have never done an honest
day's school work in their lives. Their attendance at School
is very bad indeed, and I fully expect that many of their
parents will find themselves in trouble on this matter next
term. Little or no interest shown by parents.
Evacuees. Again a different class, many of whom have missed
some months of schooling. Not nearly so intelligent as the
L.S. children, but, like them, without any ambition to work.
Their discipline is generally bad, and they make for most of
the difficulty in running the School. Their book work is
especially wretched, and they appear to be quite happy in

The "General Report and Open Letter" was sent to parents at Easter 1941. In it Mr Mallinson,
the new headmaster of Fen Drayton School, described the qualities of "Fen Drayton Natives",
"Land Settlement Children" and "Evacuees". The Report would probably not be considered
politically correct today.

In 1940 Mr Maurice Kidd, the acting Headmaster at Fen Drayton School, purchased a car for £1.00 from his uncle who lived at Wimpole. He intended that the children should dismantle it, and he constructed demonstration charts to teach them the parts of the car. Jack Wilderspin (inventor of the Jack Truck) says the unconventional lessons may well have set him on the path of his future career. Frank Parish, of Islip Farm, though he enjoyed the experience, felt more traditional subjects may well have been neglected.

62

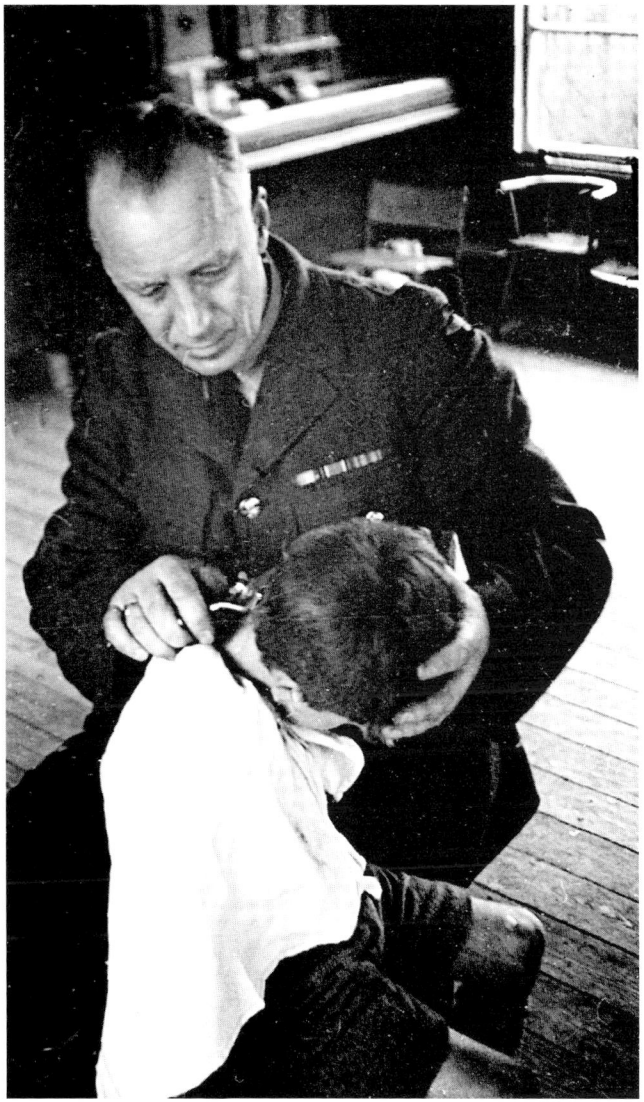

Mr S. G. Thompson taught at Fen Drayton School and also cut the boys' hair. At first in the R.A.F.V.R., he became a Squadron Leader during the war. Afterwards he returned to teach at the school once more, and remained there until retirement age.

Romance and Tragedy

The wider community continued to benefit from the sociable disposition of the settlers throughout the war. Settlers, tenants and villagers all sought to enjoy themselves whenever possible. The Three Tuns would be crammed with people intent on enjoying themselves and the beer ran out on several occasions so that someone had to be hastily sent to the Huntingdon Brewery to replenish supplies. The village hall too continued to be the focus of pleasurable activities. These included stage and cinema shows that were also enjoyed by airmen from R.A.F. Wyton. Friendly Jack Jobling took along R.A.F. friends from Oakington Airfield, where he was based. They would throw their coats into the Jobling home, then go down to the Three Tuns before joining the dancers in the village hall (sometimes Jack's friends would help to cut cabbages on his holding).

Jack Jobling was based at Oakington Airfield in Cambridgeshire during the war. He, his wife Rosemary, and his mother-in-law, look happy. They are unaware of the tragedy that will befall them before very long.

Among the visitors to the village for entertainment were four airmen from Oakington. Two officers would drive up to the Three Tuns in the front of an M.G. Sports car, with two airmen balancing on the back. The driver of the M.G. also piloted a Stirling Bomber. He was the flamboyant boyfriend of one of the Estate's Land Girls (she was said to be high class). The roar of the engines of his squadron's Stirlings as they gathered enough power to take off for their night time bombing raids on the continent, could be heard at Fen Drayton. Heavily loaded with fuel and bombs the planes flew out low over the estate at twilight. On his way back from operations, I was told, the boyfriend would fly his plane along the length of Cootes Lane in order to let the Land Girl know he was safely home. One day his plane did not return. He was missing in action.

A Stirling Bomber approaching Oakington over the railway line in 1941. Fen Drayton's inhabitants would have had a similar view of the Stirling when it flew over them. It is from this type of plane, I was told, that parcels intended for one of the Land Girls, were dropped clandestinely.

Perhaps he had a premonition because he had once had delivered to her a parcel that had amongst its contents one of his white silk scarves and a pair of flying gauntlets. I was told, and think the information true, although not corroborated because most people involved have died, that this parcel and others, had been dropped to the girlfriend from his plane to be picked up secretly in Fen Drayton. One package had to be rescued from the branches high in a tree.

The Village Hall, where couples danced to the evocative music of Glen Miller and of other composers of the time, was the birthplace of at least one romance. There, unbeknown to Bobby Carter who was on leave from the Mediterranean convoys, Jean Walker fell in love with her school days tormentor. She saw him, by then aged nineteen, at one of the weekly dances wearing his naval uniform but he was escorting someone else. Although Jean, as the result of a dare, managed to dance with Bobby in an "excuse me dance", he returned to war quite oblivious to her changed feelings towards him whilst he was participating in the bombardment of

65

Italy, and when serving on a minesweeper off Murmansk in Russia. But that is not the end of that story. I use the words "We'll Meet Again", from the poignant song Vera Lynn was singing at that time.

Within a year of war the LSA's annual loss, which had for the fifteen months ending March 1939 amounted to £42,000, had fallen to £3,546, and by 1943 the Association was solvent except in regard to interest on capital, and depreciation. A new atmosphere of optimism and relief grew on the estate. The smallholders' earnings had risen and everyone gained pleasure from knowing that they were playing a valuable part in the war effort. But these feeling were tempered when families who had hoped for a better life were hit by tragedies. John Jobling was called home from the war for the funeral of his baby brother.

Three children including Keith Jobling who was only two years old, went for a walk behind the orchards and reached the gravel pit. Doris Scutt told me a little girl became concerned about Keith and ran to tell Mrs Jobling that "Keith's gone to sleep". Keith who had a fascination with water was found lying on his side in the shallowish muddy water at the edge of the pit. Doris remembered hearing Mrs Jobling's awful screams when she realised that Keith was dead. He was her second child to die. She had left Sunderland partly because of her grief after her son Kenneth died of Diphtheria. Doris told me that Rosemary used to say of Keith, "I knew he had only been loaned to me because he had been born during the war".

Keith Jobling is sitting on the lap of Mona Dorritt a Land Army Girl who assisted Rosemary Jobling on her smallholding whilst her husband Jack was in the R.A.F.

Another tragedy followed. The teacher wrote "deceased" by David George's name in the school register on 12 July 1944. Theta Messenger remembered she was picking fruit for pocket money on the Murphy's Mill Road holding, when she heard the news of his death. David, the son of Jack who came from the Rhondda Valley, had climbed an electricity pylon and was electrocuted whilst his brother Clifford, and his young friend Ron Foster, who were looking for birds nests, watched in horror. David was only ten years old. Theta said, because they felt part of a family, everyone on the estate shared in the family's grief. I discovered that the tragedies remain prominent in people's memories to this day and especially in that of Ron Foster.

Ron had already had the great misfortune of witnessing an earlier tragedy. He was looking out of the window of his home whilst waiting for a little friend to arrive from a shopping trip, when he saw the three-year-old son of Mr and Mrs Cassidy from Durham killed when he ran into the path of a lorry. The child had run from his mother as they got off the bus opposite their home in Mill Road because he was so excited about the sweets that they had bought for Ron.

Tragically, two more sons of settlers died. Two of the boys who had so joyously ridden in Miss Chivers' Bullnose car with Bobby Carter, had their lives taken by the war. The names of Matthew (Mattie) Scott and George Finlay are carved into the village War Memorial.

On Fen Drayton's War Memorial are the names of Matthew Scott and George Finlay. They were the sons of Tom Scott, and Scott Finlay, who brought their families down from the north

Thankfully, another tragedy was narrowly averted. George, the teenager son of Tim Foster, was lucky to escape with his life whilst on the way to Kettering to help deliver LSA produce by tractor and trailer. After several miles of balancing on a bar at the back of the tractor and hanging on to the driving seat, he slipped and fell. His cries were not heard above the noise of the tractor and George was dragged for about a mile before the driver missed him and the tractor was brought to a halt. Amazingly, George recovered from his considerable injuries. His heavy army great coat had saved him.

During the war, because quite a number of trainee settlers from the Special Areas could not meet the new stringent standards imposed by the LSA, and because some of the settlers chose to leave for various other reasons, the proportion of Agricultural Tenants grew.

After the D Day Landings on 6 June 1944, it seemed that perhaps the war against Germany could indeed be won. Meanwhile, the tenants and settlers alike concentrated on the task of growing food for the nation. They continued to do so after celebrating the joyous news heard on 8 May 1945, V.E. Day, that Germany had surrendered, and even after the war was finally over the smallholders' growing regime continued as before because the food they produced was still vital to the country's economy. But before too long the estates would experience the winds of change.

Chapter 4
1945 – 1963 - Back to a Normal Life

After the war the estates were handed over to the Ministry of Agriculture and Fisheries (MAFF). They had now to fit in with the Government's aim to promote a stable and efficient agriculture as ratified in the Agricultural Act of 1947. It was considered that the smallholdings could be used to attract men to work on the land. They could provide the first rung of an "agricultural ladder" and should also be used for experiments in agricultural co-operation. The LSA would continue to manage the estates, but as the minister's agent.

An extract from the Carnegie United Kingdom Trust 35th Annual Report, 1948, states:

... The financial arrangement under the Act was that the Minister of Agriculture was empowered to take over the Association's property and in return, to remit the Association's debt to the Government. This was done ... with the good will of others who had contributed to the cost of acquiring or developing some of the property which was inherited by the Minister.

In 1974, K. J. McCready wrote as follows in "The Land Settlement Association;- Its History and Present Form" -

Thus the period of the Second World War marked the development of the Association from its pre-war role as a social experiment, to its post-war form as a collection of agricultural co-operative communities, with co-ordinated supply, production and marketing, combined to form a considerable force on the English agricultural scene.

The war's influence was still in evidence on the estate when Jim Scutt returned to Fen Drayton in 1945, to begin the new way of life that had been so abruptly postponed. He met the P.O.W.s who were helping his young wife Doris, and Richard Ahrendt, a former German Paratrooper from Hamburg who worked on the holding of Jim's brother-in-law Cyril.

Richard had moved in with the Haylers and become part of the family, even helping with the housework when Doris's sister Muriel was ill. There was also a Ukrainian P.O.W., Dennis Humeniuk, who became an LSA employee and lived at Middleton Farm.

James Brown, Tot Collier, Scott Finlay, Tim Foster, Jack Jobling, Kit Messenger, Tom Pope, Tom Scott, and Joe Watson from Chester le Street (he was the most successful settler even though he had breathing problems) were some of the remaining Special Areas settlers that Jim became acquainted with. The war had been a turning point in their fortunes, as it

c1948, Richard Ahrendt a former German Paratrooper wearing the diamond identification patch of a P.O.W. Richard was treated like one of Cyril Hayler's family and was reluctant to return to Germany but he had a wife awaiting him there. He kept in touch with the Hayler's after returning home.

c1948, German P.O.W.'s on Cyril Hayler's holding at 33 Cootes Lane. They returned home that year. Richard Ahrendt is on the right.

was for settlers on other LSA estates, and many were producing crops as fine as those of the more experienced agricultural tenants like Cyril Hayler, and had, like John Burns, paid off their loans. Others had left the LSA estates to take larger holdings elsewhere or to gain greater freedom.

Jim discovered he loved his new life in spite of a working day that could begin at 4.00 a.m. and continue until dark. He grew soft fruits, brassicas, chrysanthemums, and outdoor tomatoes for canning. His lettuces were cut early to be delivered to the packhouse by 8.00 a.m for grading and repacking. Produce, sprinkled with water to keep it fresh, was transported on barrows with a handle each end. Jim would push one and pull one. One villager described it an amazing sight when the men trundled the barrows down the road at the same time.

Jim with a two handled barrow. One villager described it an amazing sight when the men trundled the barrows at the same time. Jim proudly shows little Robert the tomatoes grown on his holding in Cootes Lane. Opposite his house are two of the style that predominates on the estate.

Although he "didn't know one end of a pig from another", Jim took up pig keeping. The LSA's centralised herd was the source of breeding sows. The profit made from livestock helped to finance the Central Farms. Jim fed his pigs on beet or barley grown by himself or animal feed purchased from R. W. Pauls whose mill was near Tower Bridge, London. When ready for slaughter the very determined and very heavy pigs would be walked through to a pen at Daintree's farm, guided with a piece of plywood. They might then be transported to Calne in Wiltshire where pigs were received from a large area for processing. One pig was saved its journey when a German P.O.W. butchered (his trade) and salted it for the Scutts.

Pigs could be a source of amusement or extreme annoyance. One day a sow escaped from her pen on Cyril Hayler's holding. With only Doris Scutt standing in a doorway between her and freedom she charged and escaped tipping Doris over into the mud as she went. On another occasion Cyril Hayler regretted hanging his jacket over the side of the pen containing fattening pigs because later he discovered its remnants spread in the mud in the bottom of the pen. He was less upset about the loss of the

71

In 1947 Doris Scutt with baby Robert at 31 Cootes Lane. The
semi-detached houses in the background are numbered 38 to 50
Middleton Way. Marrows are growing in the foreground.

jacket than by the loss of the pouch of tobacco that had been in its pocket. Theta Messenger found to her cost that other people's pigs could be her undoing. She used to pick up her bike from a friend's house after returning late after an evening in St Ives, and would cycle home along the lanes in the dark without switching the bike's lights on. One day, she collided with an escaped pig (one of Jim's?) and was catapulted head over heels into the sprout crop.

Theta had ridden without lights because she was afraid of tramps. Tramps would often be discovered, with the aid of Hurricane lamps, huddled around the fire hole near the furnace for the glasshouse on the holdings. Theta was told that they left a secret sign to indicate to others suitable places to visit. She said her mother would give them a cup of tea and crusts, and kind hearted Mrs Williams next door, despite having five children to provide for, would give them a cooked meal. No doubt the tramps would remember this.

Jim and his fellows experienced a particularly testing time during the especially severe winter of 1947. Extremely deep falls of snow became frozen preventing anyone from working on their land for weeks while all around them wild birds, ducks, and geese lay dying from starvation. But the smallholders were threatened with the possibility of an even greater disaster when the snow thawed suddenly and rapidly, for Fen Drayton lay in close proximity to Over on the River Great Ouse. It was there that the swollen river breached its banks to inundate a vast area of the surrounding low-lying land and caused widespread destruction. But amazingly, for the most part, the Estate escaped the floods although many village properties were flooded. Tenants sighed with relief.

That same year Jim and Doris had another very good reason to give thanks. Their toddler son Robert loved to perch in a wooden tray fastened to the handle of a "Trusty Tractor" while his father drove it along. Unfortunately when the tray became loose Jim delayed re-attaching it to the handle. One day it slipped, tipping Robert over the side of the tractor down towards the rotavator blades. He was only inches from being crushed when Jim, his heart in his stomach, hooked Robert sideways to safety with the toe of his boot. The tray was very quickly made secure.

In November, the Royal Wedding between Princess Elizabeth and Philip Mountbatten was celebrated. It was an eventful year.

Disaster threatens the LSA Estate. The River Great Ouse has breached its banks at Over. On 18 March 1947 the floodwater surged onto holdings in Oak Tree Road and Springhill Road. In the distance to the left of the picture is Holywell and to the right is Over. In the centre the faint line running diagonally from left to right reveals the route of the Huntingdon to Cambridge railway.

In 1948, young Robert Scutt is perched on a tray on the Trusty tractor while Dad Jim is discing ploughed ground to make a fine tilth. Behind are Cootes Lane houses, and piggeries that have a tool shed at the ends and two pens each side.

c1950, the Combine Harvester has been hired by the LSA to harvest the barley grown by the tenants to feed to their pigs.
I to r: Frank Berry, a villager, John Jobling (son of Jack), Fred 'Dickie' Darlow who was Sam Johnson's (the farmer) tractor driver, Jim Scutt and Ivor Pope (son of Tom from the Rhondda).

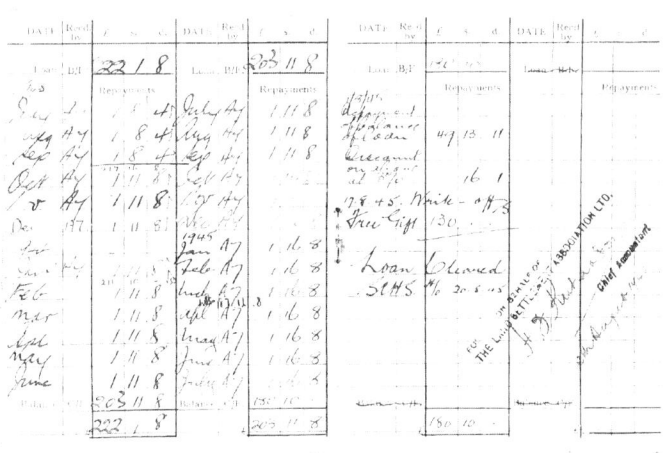

A page of the Tenants Pass Book given to Bill Laverick when he began his tenancy after completing his training in October 1940. It records the repayment of the loan he was given by the LSA. On 17 August 1945 an entry states "Write off Free Gift, £130". 20 August 1945 was a momentous day for him when his LSA loan was finally recorded as cleared.

Discontent and Rule Breaking

Tenants returned from the war in a more independent state of mind. Following the report of a committee chaired by Mr George Brown, Parliamentary Secretary to the Ministry in 1948, from 1951 they gained the right to hold their smallholdings on annual tenancy agreements rather than 364 day lettings. This provided them with security of tenure and entitlement to compensation when quitting. They were also given the possibility of a say in LSA policy through estate committees, and a tenants' central consultative association. These changes were not considered enough by some.

Although LSA tenants were provided with good land, loans for ensuring efficient capitalisation, good quality plants, technical advice and services, and the benefits of bulk buying, they found the rules too constraining, as did Tom Pope from the Rhondda. He resented not being able to find his own markets particularly when he was ordered to dump tons of tomatoes for lack of demand. Nevertheless an enterprising man like Tom could adopt an unorthodox way of dealing with certain restrictions. For example, as an excuse for having wrung its neck he would tell the warden, in his Welsh accent, that a missing hen had been put in the pot "because it looked a bit fragile".

Like Tom, Richard Gash, a later arrival, also disliked the restrictions. He left his Mill Road holding after seven years, in 1958, to buy a smallholding from the Co-op at Willingham, on which he built a house. Before that, his wife explained to me, he too had indulged in illicit selling. She called it "boot legging". For example, he sold anemones, a cash crop, to a greengrocer in Crown Street, St Ives. She said there was a lot of illicit selling in the 1950s, and that everyone did it because Mr Scott the Estate Manager couldn't prove it, and couldn't catch those involved.

Robert Scutt said he earned pocket money on the holdings by making up "Filmers" (cardboard baskets), and Richard's daughter Brenda weeded carrots and onions for one penny a row to save half towards the cost of a bike, but her sister Joyce thought money was insufficient incentive. She refused Richard's offer of work to help finance a school trip saying she didn't want to work herself to death just to go on an outing.

One day in the 1960's, Jim stood chatting with Stan Livett of holding No. 42 on the service path crossing the holdings where they were joined by Dick

1949 - A Job well done. Potatoes loaded ready for delivery to the market.
l to r: Mrs Ingle, Beryl Williams, Theta Messenger, Alan Coe (the driver), Mrs Stuking and Mrs McDermot

c1946 Three friends who enjoy life on the estate. Theta Messenger from Esh Winning, Betty Heath from West Hartlepool and Gladys Nutall from Thornley, Co. Durham.

78

Lockwood of No. 30. The men began to compare their clothes. Jim was wearing a scruffy rain coat which had been badly torn by a pig and was held together by wire instead of stitching; Dick Lockwood was tied about with string and rope, and because of a missing button, Stan's braces were wired to the top of his trousers. They decided that they looked like real "country oiks". But perhaps they were practising for a future event. We shall see!

Strong winds would hit the estate. One day Tom Juf's glass, four Dutch lights set on straw bales or railway sleepers, with a head height of 6' 6", was not securely wired down. While Jim Scutt was helping his neighbour to repair it one gusty day Tom left to get another piece of glass. Luckily Jim also moved away because a violent gust smashed the glasshouse down with a great crash. Fortunately a neighbour was able to reassure an anxious Doris Scutt who had heard the noise, that Jim and Tom were safe. The lettuce crop was totally ruined. In November 1957 gales did far more serious damage in the area. Mr Hunter a new arrival at that time explains:

"The winds were of such severity the swinging of the overhead electric cables caused the poles to tilt over. Even the water in the S-trap of the loo was sucked out. Needless to say the damage to the glasshouses was extensive. It was fortunate that the gale happened at night. ... by morning the wind had lessened and all that could be heard was the sound of crashing glass as people tried to clear up. All credit to the LSA for, straight away, replacement glass was being delivered. ...There were stories of some of the pig houses being blown over with the pigs inside. I don't know of any injuries but some were none too pleased to be trapped."

Foxes were yet another problem for smallholders to contend with. Another form of disaster took place for a Mr Clarke when a fox decimated a flock of two or three hundred hens when it got beneath the slatted floors of a poultry shed. Jim said it did it just for the sake of it.

Many tenants kept hens. Alan Hunter wrote about the effect on the estate when Fowl Pest was confirmed in the area.

"....all poultry on the estate had to be culled. ... We worked round, holding by holding. Every time it was the same; frightened noisy birds fluttering round, the quiet when we left. My wife and I had, what was in those days, a commercial flock which I would visit each evening, the scuffling, the gentle clucking until the cull and then the awful silence".

Joe Higgins with the steam sterilizer, which was used to sterilize the soil in the glasshouses. Mischievous children dared each other to climb into it while it lay on its side after being cleaned.

1957 Picking Tomatoes - Richard Gash and his family who had arrived from Nottingham in 1951. They remained on their Mill Road holding for 22 years. Estate children helped on the holdings from an early age. Some more willingly than others.

On Alan Hunter's holding at 14 Cootes Lane, in August 1958, stands a Dutch-light glasshouse by Westdock Timber Company of Hull. Next to it is the smaller Landlord's (LSA's) glasshouse, which has chrysanthemums in pots lined up beside it.

c1959 and Robert Scutt is no longer small enough to perch on the Trusty Tractor to watch while Dad works. He is now a great help to Jim.

Alan Hunter is tending his flock of hens at No. 14 Cootes Lane. Most tenants had either pigs or poultry, or both, in addition to horticultural crops, until the smallholders were asked to concentrate on horticulture alone.

The chrysanthemum crop on Alan Hunter's holding. Once the tomato season was over a mobile house was brought to cover the flowers as they would need protection from frost. Alan wrote: "The days leading to Christmas were busier than ever, getting the chrysanthemums away before the holiday . Not that there was much of a holiday even when there was no livestock, the break was little more than a few hours off on Christmas Day and Boxing Day afternoons. When we took over the holding, the winter was reckoned as a time to take things easier. As the years went on this easier time grew less and less until it disappeared altogether. Night by night the lamps glowed in the greenhouses as preparations for the coming season were made".

Day old chicks were supplied to the estates from the LSA's central hatchery. Alan Hunter's, Rhode Island Red x Light Sussex, chickens, are in a Hover. It contains a paraffin lamp to keep them warm. The chickens were easy to sex because the hens took on the colour of the cockerel (Rhode Island Red).

"Moneymaker" tomatoes - Alan Hunter hopes so !

Social Life on the estate continues

It was not all work and no play. As ever the men enjoyed themselves at the Three Tuns. Charlie Giddings the horse man sang rude songs, and responding to calls of "Come on Edmund", Edmund Furness a local builder sang "Do You Ken John Peel". Among them was Tom Burton, the man who mended bicycles. Tom was a village character known for his habit of cycling with a pet hen nestling in the basket on the front of his bike and for sitting on his permanently "reserved" seat in the pub while the hen perched on the back of a chair.

LSA Tenants Association charabanc outing to Hunstanton 1949.
l to r : Cyril Hayler, with Robert Scutt and his teddy bear, stand next to Leonard & Agnes Goddard and their daughter Eileen, Mr & Mrs Missen with two of their children, are next to George Butler (in blazer), and Peter Benson, Bill Adams in his cap stands next to Rose Carter. They are behind Albert Carter a village child, and John Posey. May & Les Wright are in the group behind Douglas & John Missen who are clutching seaside buckets. Others unknown.

Babs Burns, the "townie", spoke of "plenty going on" including day trips to Hunstanton. She described how mothers would push prams and wheelbarrows containing children, the long way round by road to Swavesey Station, because the short-cut by track was too narrow for prams to pass through. And then how they returned by the same route after a tiring day to rise early next morning to begin work with their bodies aching all over.

A tramps supper provided great amusement and brought out people's competitive streak. They competed to look the most realistic (remember Jim Scutt and Stan Livett had had much practice) so much so, that a worried visitor to the Three Tuns commented to Bert Culmer, the new landlord, on the fact that his village was very full of rough tramp types that evening. The publican reassured him that they were harmless if left alone.

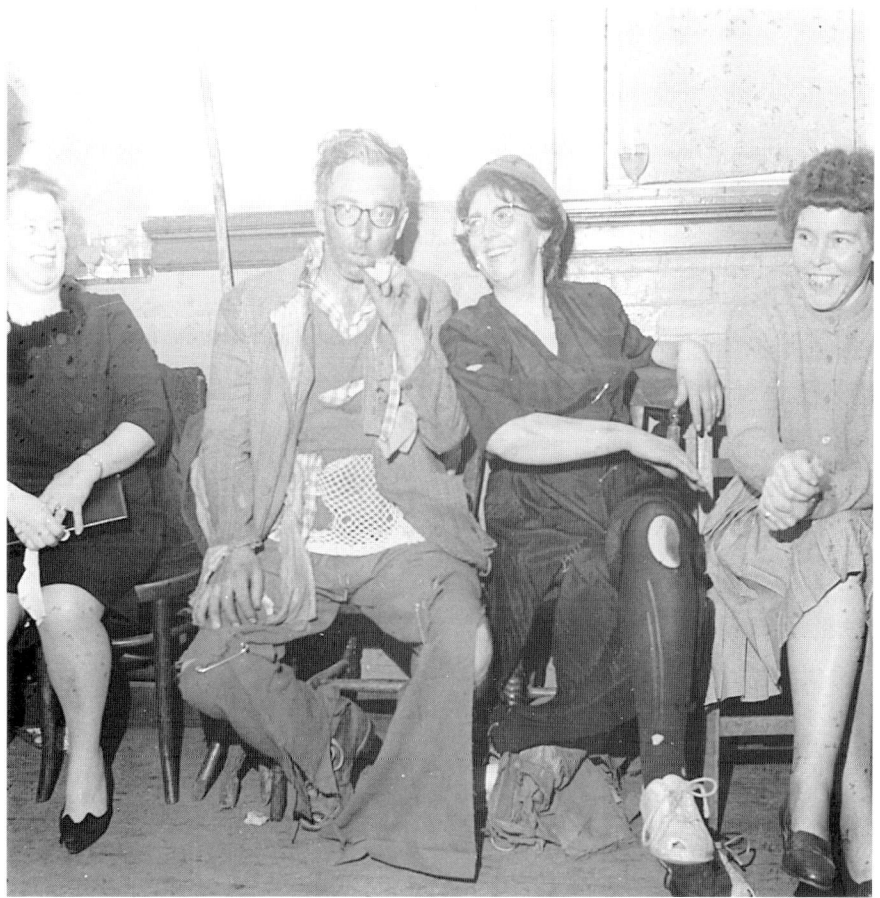

c1965 - "Harmless if left alone".
Stan and Dorothy Livett of 42 Middleton Way look the part at the Tramps Evening held at Fen Drayton Village Hall. No wonder a visitor to the village expressed his concern to Bert Culmer, landlord of the Three Tuns, about the rough looking people in the village that night.

Pram Race, 31 December 1965. The Independent Press said, "The race organised by the newly-formed Social Club, was won by Mr Brian Grey (pushing) and by Mr George Burton (riding). Money raised will go towards a New Year's Day party for the village's 137 children."

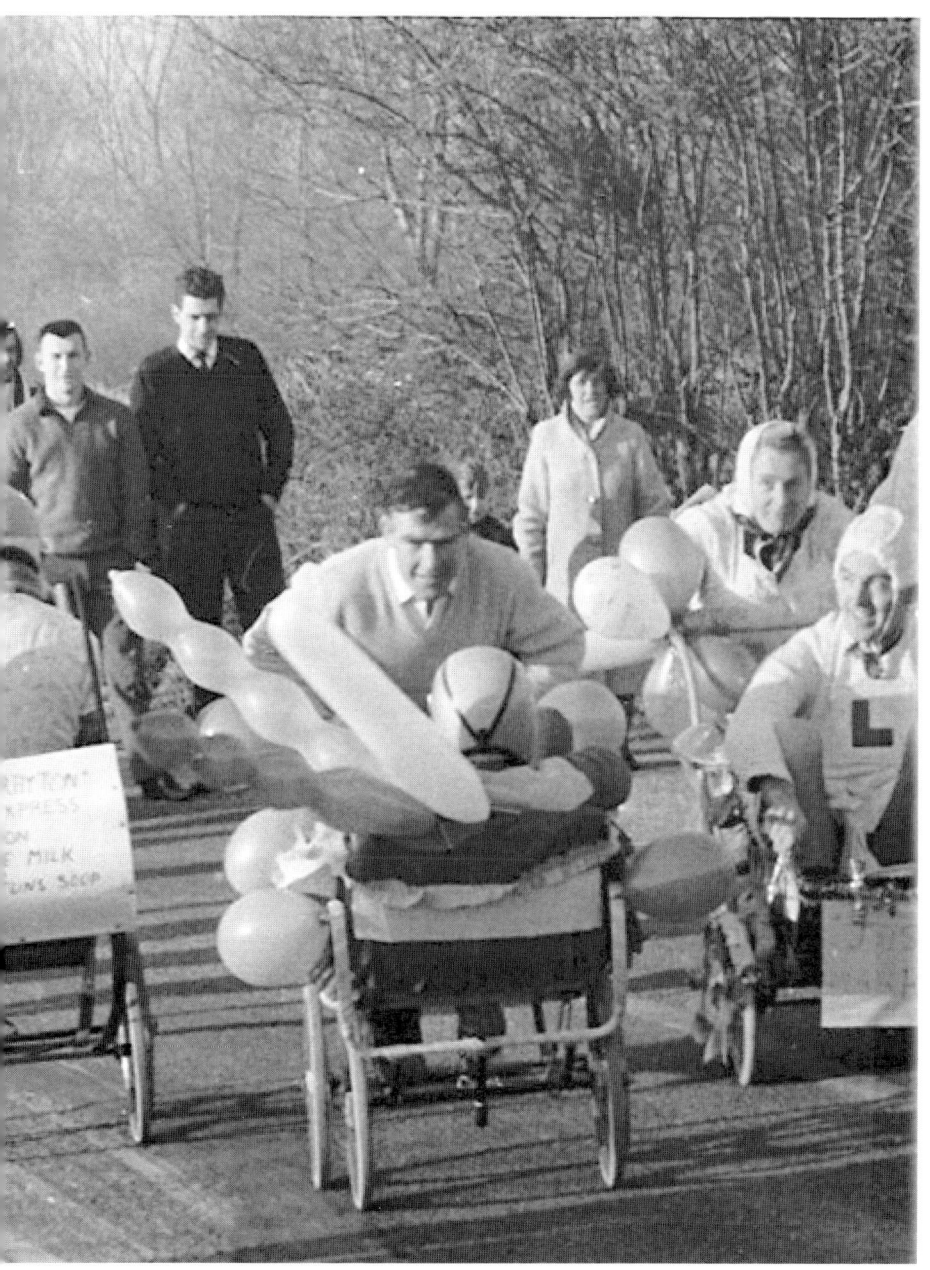

Another opportunity to dress up was provided by an annual pram race, when men dressed in women's clothes raced down Mill Road with their skirts flapping, and pushing overgrown babies in their prams. The race provided a great source of amusement and hilarity for several years until the police banned it for safety reasons.

Boxing Day c 1966   -   In best pram racing garb. Geoffrey D'Alcorn of Cootes Lane and George Butler.

A Frosty Day for the Annual Pram Race. The race was a great source of amusement and hilarity for several years until the police stopped it for safety reasons.

There were a variety of sports groups in which villagers and smallholders participated. The events provided extra opportunities for romances, of which there were many, including those in the Carter family. Rose, who as a little girl rode Betsy pig, fell in love with and married Herbie Burgess, a local farmer, her sister Barbara fell in love with Pip Gill the propagating officer, and Bobby fell in love with, whom do you think?

Bobby Carter, Jean Walker's childhood tormentor, after being demobilised in 1946, saw Jean's brother at an event at the Corn Exchange in St Ives, and enquired after her. The brother gave Bobby a photo of Jean he had carried in the war and Bobby plucked up courage to visit K's shoe shop in St Ives where Jean worked, to ask her for a date, but instead bought a pair of shoes. Lovesick Jean would take a detour, on her bike, to her home in Swavesey, via Fen Drayton, just to wave to him. Love blossomed. Three years later they married and lived happily ever after.

"What a Surprise" - Bobby Carter and Jean Walker were married in 1950, 25 years after they crossed swords at Swavesey School. They lived happily ever after - as the storybooks say. l to r: Rose Carter, Pip Gill, Connie Levell, Bobby Carter, Jean Carter, Fred Walker (Jean's brother), Betty Walker (Jean's sister)

There were also marriages between the villagers and the incomers, including that between Isla McDermot, daughter of Mrs 'Mac' former housekeeper at Fen Drayton House, and Billy Hannah the tractor driver son of a tenant.

Scout and guide groups provided fun for younger children as did the youth club and the many activities arranged by Mr Thompson the schoolmaster. He would take boys fishing and on various visits, and he would let them use the tools in his work-shop. Most excitingly he bought an ML 292 motor torpedo boat from the Admiralty with the intention of taking parties of girls and boys on trips. Ron Foster explained how he and two mates accompanied Mr Thompson to Gillingham Docks to help prepare it for use. Depth charge tubes and other equipment were removed and Royal Navy markings painted out. Then with an engineer on board they sailed into London and then to a mooring at Oulton Broad in Norfolk. What a great adventure for a child.

Teacher, Squadron Leader Thompson, moored his ML 292 Motor Torpedo Boat at Oulton Broad in Norfolk. Fen Drayton school children and youth groups were taken there on outings. l to r: Lilly Scott, from Sunderland, Gladys Nutall, from Co. Durham, Connie Pope from The Rhondda, and Billy Laverick from Sunderland.

Pastures new

Although the LSA's policies were formulated with an increasing emphasis on commercial criteria, its paternalistic caring side continued. For example, men who gave up their holdings, voluntarily or otherwise, were given occupations on the estates, or were able to retire to cottages without land at Yeldham Estate in Essex. William Williams and Jack George, two of the Welsh settlers, moved there in 1947 and 1948.

C1959, Lorries are leaving the packing shed at Middleton Farm in Cootes Lane to transport graded lettuces to the market.

Of the 17 northerners photographed in 1936, on a visit to Unwins, many had vacated their holdings by the end of the war and some left soon afterwards. Early leavers included George Parr who returned north, Walter Messenger who stayed locally, Mr Abernethy who returned to the north, Tommy Lumley returned to the north then returned back to the south, Mr ?Tom Johnson returned north, Harry Sawyer settled in Fenstanton (he gave one of the best sermons ever heard at its Methodist Chapel, said Jack Dady, local historian), Ted Harrison left during the war and Joby Nutall possibly returned north in the 1940s. Bob Carter vacated his holding to go north to the shipyards during the war but, as you will have noted, he and the family also settled in the south.

In the May 20 1950 edition of "The Grower", it was stated that there were about ten of the total original settlers remaining at Fen Drayton. These would have included Tot Collier, Jack Jobling, Tim Foster, Mr Brown, Kit Messenger and possibly Scott Finlay who stayed until at least 1947.

Very few from the Special Areas continued cultivating until retirement age so very few remained into the 1960's. Some had chosen new ventures locally, others had been given ultimatums by their wives. William Laverick from Sunderland was persuaded by his dressmaker wife to give up his holding. She regretted this later because he wasn't happy in successive jobs. Tot Collier from Perkinsville, County Durham, vacated his holding at retirement age in the 1950s. Pagebank's Tim Foster stayed until retiring at the age of sixty in 1960, to buy a house with land in the village of Over and Kit Messenger from Esh Winning stayed on his holding until forced to retire in 1962, after 27 years at Middleton Way, because he was aged 70. He went to live with his son-in-law and daughter Theta on their smallholding in Hemingford Grey.

Tom Pope, one of the Welsh settlers, was another who stayed until retirement age. In 1964 he moved to a council house in Fen Drayton close to the Burns family. John Burns had vacated his holding in 1947 (he was another who had received an ultimatum from his wife), because a pregnant Babs refused to bring up another child on the settlement.

The family eventually acquired a council house newly built on the site of Fen Drayton House Plantation and Mrs Burns went back to nursing and did all the laying out in the village. Her

Babs had said she couldn't tell a weed from a blade of grass. She rather proved her assertion by pulling out the carrots, and not the weeds, from the carrot bed.

husband worked as a pasteurizer at Keith Wright's Dairy at Fenstanton, now "Dairycrest". As we have seen many who left the LSA found work at the Dairy including Bob Carter when he returned from the shipyard after the war. Only two families' descendents would carry on with the smallholding life, as we shall see later.

Fen Drayton's estate became a showcase for the LSA with visitors from Algeria, Uganda, Turkey, India, Korea and elsewhere. Mr Piper used to guide them to view Rosemary Jobling's house, for she was known for her rigid housework routine and would be sure to have sparkling windows. The LSA Scheme received frequent and favourable publicity in the national and farming press.

A Department Committee of Inquiry into Statutory Smallholdings begun in 1963 and chaired by Professor M. J. Wise, would report on the LSA in 1967:

"It has attracted attention all over the world as a unique example of a form of co-operation. Representatives of the Association have visited emergent nations to advise their Governments on land settlement. The Association's Annual Report for 1959/60 refers to the favourable view of the Scheme formed by the Director General of the Food and Agriculture Organisation of the United Nations after he had paid a visit to an LSA estate" ... *"I believe (The Association) has an interesting lesson for many countries ... in developing a prosperous peasant economy without, at the same time, destroying individual incentives for production and profit".*

Throughout this period a process of gradual change was under way on the holdings. Fruit growing was phased out and fewer root vegetables and brassica crops were grown. Farmyard noises were diminishing, as were pungent smells, as tenants gave up pig and poultry keeping. The LSA was again entering a new phase.

AN EXPERIMENT IN
SMALLHOLDINGS

Conducted by THE LAND SETTLEMENT ASSOCIATION LTD

4 3   C r o m w e l l   R o a d ,   L o n d o n ,   S . W . 7

Price Two Shillings

This attractive design was on the cover of a booklet entitled, "An Experiment in Smallholdings", published c1948, and also on another entitled, "Smallholdings with Marketing and other Services", produced in 1959 for the Association's Silver Jubilee. It is a rather romantic depiction of an estate with crops and animals shown in healthy abundance. Before long the animals would be gone from the estates.

94

Chapter 5
Mid 1960s – 1982
The End of the Three-Legged Stool

By the mid 1960s the number of LSA holdings was down from the original 1040 to about 525, and there would soon be even fewer.

In 1963 the Minister of Agriculture and Fisheries of the incoming Conservative Government had appointed a committee under the Chairmanship of Professor M. J. Wise to examine all aspects of the LSA Organisation. The Wise Report, published in 1967, ushered in yet another new chapter for the smallholding estates.

Professor Wise advised the Minister that there was no longer a need for the national scheme, certainly not in its present form, but that the Ministry had an obligation to those already in it. The Minister decided the scheme would continue but accepted that the compulsory use of the centralised services should be eased. He agreed also that commercial horticulture be intensified, with greater specialisation in salad production, and that those estates that could not adapt to the new regime should be withdrawn. His decision marked the end of the LSA's policy "that diversity on the holdings provides security", the "three legged stool" of horticulture, pigs and poultry. Only ten estates of the eighteen remaining after the war were suitable for horticultural production. Fen Drayton was one of them.

After the Wise Report in 1967, only 10 estates were considered suitable for concentrated horticultural production and could stay in the LSA scheme

Billy Hannah an LSA driver (his father was a tenant), and Alan Coe, are loading chicken
trays, each containing 15 lettuces, to be delivered to the packing shed for repacking.

In fact, the four northern livestock estates had already been closed and
poultry and pig keeping on all the estates was gradually being phased out
as they became unprofitable because of increasing competition. The last
boar left Fen Drayton in 1966.

Improved crop protection was needed for the greater specialisation in
horticulture. Growers invested in a wooden-framed glasshouse called the
"Fen Structure", which Tom Scott, Fen Drayton's manager, had developed
with Gabriel Wade and English of Ipswich. It could be combined as a
multi-bay to measure 100ft square.

The LSA experimented with mobile glasshouses. With a span of 40ft x
100ft they were set on a central and two side rails. Weighing about seven
tons and designed to be towed by tractor over two or three stations (plots),
they were more easily moved manually by a gang of men. Roger Robinson
explained that he and his neighbours in Mill Road would set a day aside
for this task. They would begin pushing early in the morning at No. 1 then
progress onto neighbouring holdings in succession throughout the

day, until the mobile on No. 10 was safely repositioned. The mobiles were relocated with the seasons to protect different crops. Early in the year lettuces would be given protection until it was time for the mobile to be moved to new ground for tomatoes to be planted beneath. After the lettuces had been cut, chrysanthemums might be planted in their place and the glasshouse returned to cover them once the tomato season was over. LSA growers were also in the forefront of experimentation with low-cost production techniques, including the use of polythene tunnels.

Chrysanthemums grown by Leonard and Agnes Goddard. They lived at holding No. 21 Oak Tree Road for five years from about 1948 before leaving the LSA for a smallholding at Hemingford Grey.

Steamy goings on

Greenhouses provided opportunities for unusual activities. On one estate polytunnels were lined with black polythene to create the hot, dark and steamy conditions required for the forcing of rhubarb. The rhubarb was cut with the aid of lighted candles propped on sticks. The resulting shadowy interiors provided an ideal setting for hotter and steamier behaviour than cutting rhubarb. So related one manager to another, saying that he kept a record of such things he learned of. He spoke too of a Fen Drayton tenant who had been seen having illicit amorous relations with a lady in his glasshouse. The tenant was oblivious to the fact that his tomato plants were not sufficiently dense to hide the activities from his neighbour's view.

The more ambitious tenants invested in large oil-heated "Venlo" glasshouses (a type that had originated in Holland), which could cover either a tenth or a quarter of an acre. They had galvanised iron frames with aluminium roofing bars and ridges. Light and airy, they provided a permanent controlled environment in which to grow cheap, clean, unblemished salads all the year round as required by the supermarkets.

1976 aerial photograph of Nos. 42, 43, 44 and 45 Middleton Way. The dominant feature on Ian Ruggles's holding at No. 44, is the Venlo glasshouse, a type which originated in Holland. It could cover either a tenth or a quarter of an acre. Above it are two sets of mobile glasshouses and then open ground to which they were moved along runners with the seasons.

Ian Ruggles arrived on the estate in the 1960s after working in the glasshouse industry. An aerial photograph of Middleton Way taken in the early 1970s, shows how his holding (second from the right) reflected the changes. On it the most dominant feature is the Venlo glasshouse. A service road, used by delivery vehicles, can be seen running horizontally across the picture immediately behind the first glasshouses. A timber pig house and two small LSA glasshouses, known as the landlord's (LSA's), face the track. Immediately behind the piggery is a circular metal free-

99

standing, 5,000 gallon reservoir, which was installed in 1970. Behind the reservoir is a Fenland Structure. Above the Venlo house in the top half of the photograph are the Dutchlight mobiles set on concrete dollies with wheels. Behind them it can be seen that the plot is divided into two more sections 100ft long x 60ft to accommodate the mobiles at different times of the year.

There were 34 acres of glass on Fen Drayton's estate by the end of 1973, the third highest average of glass per holding in the Association. Philip Hamlett the former manager has lasting memories of installing more and more glass, which he explained, "enabled the round lettuce to become the battery egg of the horticultural world". By 1971 there were 17 acres of celery under glass. The celery was washed and packed into polythene sleeves by the tenants. Some tenants grew either lettuce or tomatoes. The installation of glass continued.

By 1972 the tenants were referred to as Growers and preferred recruits were young men in their late twenties with at least five years agricultural or horticultural experience. This could include three years at College, but Philip Hamlett had found that the ordinary land labourer with a feeling for the soil could excel, and that former herdsmen like Ernest Leech of 49 Middleton Way, and John Cox of 5 Mill Road, were particularly successful. College experience and degrees certainly did not guarantee success. The livelihood and mental health of one Fen Drayton tenant deteriorated disastrously and he went bankrupt, after his son became involved in the running of the holding after a horticultural education.

I was amused to hear how one young man was turned down by Siddlesham's Estate Manager because he had no money and no wife. In a very short time he re-applied successfully for a holding. He had the money, he had a wife, and the wife was already expecting a baby.

It was accepted by 1974 that the producer must grow what the customer wished to buy. This included lettuce, tomatoes, cucumbers, peppers and self-blanching celery. The responsibility for finding outlets for all the produce gradually passed from the estates' managers to the Association's Marketing Officer. He contacted the main buyers and then visited the estates to try to match demand with timing, quality and quantity, and he could request that a tenant change his acreage. Some Fen Drayton growers preferred the old system. They say their profitability fell with the change to central marketing. They also continued to be disgruntled about the cost of central purchasing.

1972 Aerial photograph of part of Fen Drayton Estate. The Estate's Central Farm is in the foreground with its large propagating unit to the right. There were also facilities provided for handling flowers. Fen Drayton was one of the few LSA Estates with these facilities. The Middleton Way holdings stretch upwards on the right, away from those in Cootes Lane. As time went on more and more glass was added to the holdings and fewer crops grown in the open ground. Older growers were unhappy about the increasing commercialisation of the growing regime and the increasing competitiveness of fellow growers.
(Copyright reserved Cambridge University Collection of Air Photographs)

Professor Wise had reported in 1967:

The Centralised Services were for many a cause of a variety of grievances ... The main burden of grievance, was that the LSA prices were no cheaper or at times in the case of some commodities, dearer than tenants would pay if they bought their requisites from local suppliers.

It appears there was some justification for the complaints. Derek Tuck, former Service Department Manager at Fen Drayton, said he discovered he could sometimes have bought cheaper oil outside the organisation.

In spite of its problems the LSA had many successes. Philip Hamlett said it led the field in providing produce for supermarkets, pioneering and developing direct sales from the 1950s. He said it was the only organisation large enough to do so in 1956, when it supplied the International Stores. It also pioneered the concept of non-returnable trays for moving produce. By the 1960s, Fen Drayton's Estate supplied a large proportion of its produce to J. Sainsbury, for whom it experimented with new crops, including peppers and cherry tomatoes, and it experimented with the pre-packaging of beans and was the first to pack lettuces into plastic bags. The LSA also supplied Marks and Spencer, which demanded the best quality and like other firms rejected produce not of a uniform size. Not until the early 1970s was there any other organisation large enough to join in. The LSA also developed and encouraged the introduction of new techniques.

Roger Robinson was among those who embraced new techniques. Roger, from a farming background, sought to make his enterprise as efficient as possible. As mentioned previously, he took over No. 8 Mill Road in 1961 in which he invested £16,000 over time to increase his glass area from 5,000 sq ft to 60,000 sq ft. He hired an LSA spading machine which worked like a rotavator and also a lettuce planting machine, and was the first on the estate to buy a "Jack Truck" pallet lifter, and first to have a block planting machine. This formed blocks from soil or peat and inserted a seed in them ready for planting. He also had a special packhouse on his holding in which his cut chrysanthemums could take up water over-night before transportation to Covent Garden. He later found it more profitable to have four follow-on crops of lettuce. In the 1970's Roger was growing more than 12,000 plants, 6,000 in one glasshouse, and he employed three full-time men and some casual workers. He said, for example, that tomatoes were very labour intensive and he needed paid labour to cope with the removal of side shoots.

Fen Drayton tenants had begun to employ labour on the holdings from the late 1950s and then increasingly so from the surrounding villages. By 1971 casual and permanent labour came from as far as the Chatteris area in the Fens. There could be 40 or 50 people working in the packhouse seasonally.

Roger Robinson of Mill Road with the hired Lettuce Planting Machine. Two people sat on the machine to do the planting while another steered and supplied them with lettuce plants growing in blocks of soil. Find the hidden person...

Maurice Lanchebury used a wooden rake with tines eight inches apart to mark out squares. His wife planted the lettuces into the squares by hand. She said she and her husband liked working together. But I learned that the relationships of some couples were severely tested by the problems they faced in the growing way of life, and that they might work together in moody silence for many hours. Some marriages fell apart.

103

Community Tensions

As horticultural production under glass expanded so the smallholders' working hours increased. Because there were no longer quiet periods there was even less time available for the villagers and the growing community to mix socially to make friends. The growing fraternity bonded because of their shared daily experiences. For example, the women would turn to each other for advice on such things as how to cope with the very severe and painful problem of celery rash (topics which were of no interest to villagers). They felt separate from and looked down upon by the villagers. One parent thought a village schoolteacher was prejudiced against "settlement" children, lumping them together as "thick", and wrongly accused parents of not giving them enough support (numbers of children went on to a college or university education). It seems that settlers too felt there was some stigma attached to being of the settlement, for at least one daughter of a settler pictured on the Unwins photograph did not wish to acknowledge her origins once the family moved off it. Her sister, living locally and comfortably, still chooses to forget that the family went through a bad patch long ago in Durham.

A Fen Drayton farmer told me there were mixed feelings about the estate dwellers, with some locals totally against them. Here is one example of the tensions between the two communities. I was told by a manager that in the 1960s the placing of the Village Hall so close to the Central Farm was much regretted by the LSA. Delivery lorries were by this time 30ft-40ft long, and were experiencing great difficulty when turning in the cramped space between the packing shed and central stores, and a cottage and the Village Hall. But the Village Hall Management Committee, wary of the LSA's motives, would not allow the manager to gravel an area close to the hall to create better access for the vehicles although it would also have provided a car park for the Village Hall. Instead, so I was told, it erected a rough fence of halved railway sleeper posts to stop any vehicles encroaching on the area. The LSA did not solve the access problem until the 1970s, when it demolished the cottage to achieve the required space for the increasingly large vehicles. Sometimes, there would be as many as ten Sainsbury's delivery vehicles queuing at the packing shed at one time.

Some villagers took advantage of the presence of the estate, for not only did it provide jobs and social activities but it also provided customers for the village store, the Post Office and the engineering business of Jack Wilderspin. Jack had set up his business at College Farm (the family farm) from where he provided a welding and engineering service for the tenants. In 1968 he noticed that, unusually, produce had been packed into pallets on the holdings and the pallets had been stacked at the roadside for direct delivery to the markets. He understood that this was because of a head office directive. Because a tenant said he was coping with them with great difficulty, Jack designed and produced the "Jacktruck", a hydraulic pallet transporter, which enabled the handling of a large number of pallets with ease. Able to lift up to half a ton, it revolutionised the handling of pallets on the estate. Profits from sales of these unique pallet transporters, mainly to LSA estates, contributed to the success and expansion of his business.

A number of Fen Drayton's tenants moved to County Council owned smallholdings, including those at Girton, Willingham, and Over, where they hoped for greater freedom. By the 1970s and 80s, on only three holdings were there links to the early settlers. Jack Jobling's son John took over the tenancy of 34 Cootes Lane in 1963 when his father, who came from Sunderland, retired after 28 years on the holding. But John died, so his wife Sadie (she had met John when on a visit to her own Sunderland relatives on the settlement) took over the tenancy, only the second woman allowed to do so by the LSA, and she was followed by Jack's grandson Keith, who took over in 1979. Jack continued to advise and help on the holding until he died aged 89 in 1987.

Bob Carter's daughter ensured another link was kept with the original settlers when she married Pip Gill, the Estate's propagating officer and their son Neville was born. Pip acquired a holding in Cootes Lane and became noted for his chrysanthemum growing. With Barbara, he would produce 30,000 boxes of the colourful blooms in the three month season. Later, Neville acquired the neighbouring holding and he too produced large quantities of flowers.

Besides the addition of glasshouses Fen Drayton's landscape reflected other changing requirements of the LSA. At the central farm area a new pack-house was built in 1946, and in 1967 a propagating unit, 140ft x 210 ft, was erected which was needed to produce sufficient quantities of high quality, disease free plants that were unobtainable elsewhere. Also a cold storage unit for storing cut flowers was provided. Fen Drayton's estate was one of only a few in the Association fully equipped to handle flowers. In the vicinity of Fen Drayton House in the 1940s, an orchard was sold and replaced by "The Orchard" council houses, and in the 1950s the House itself was adapted into flats for the Estate Manager and LSA staff. In 1956

The JACKTRUCK
Patent No.
1285331

up to 500 kg loaded pallet transporter

The photograph shows the Jacktruck being used with a Honda, it can be towed by a variety of small tractors or rotavators which together make up the complete unit.

Simple to load:

Lower the frame, lift off wheel assembly reverse truck under pallets.

Lay the wheel assembly in position and pump up the frame.

The unit is then ready to move off complete with load.

Simple to unload:

Lower the frame and lift off the wheel assembly.

Move the unit forward, replace the wheel assembly and pump up the frame.

Move off and proceed to collect another load.

In 1968 Jack Wilderspin, who was from a local farming family and had once attended the village school, invented an hydraulic pallet transporter. Its unique method of lowering three inches for the loading fork to be inserted under the pallets was of great assistance to the growers. The sales of over 200 Jacktrucks to growers at Fox Ash, Abington, Wyboston and Newent Estates, boosted the growth of his business which also maintained the Honda tractors which towed them.

I was told that a Japanese visitor photographed the other visitors to Fen Drayton Estate. They were looking at the Jacktruck in use on Roger Robinson's holding. Roger said he had been glad the LSA had provided him with the opportunity to start his own business. Roger and others on the estate employed paid labour. Fen Drayton's tenants were the first to employ full-time help outside the family.

two houses were built in Cootes Lane for LSA staff. The LSA sold surplus land for a new village school that was opened at Easter 1971, and for "The Plantation" local authority houses which replaced mixed ornamental woodland. The woodland had already been damaged by foraging pigs. In the 1970s, in the area known as the Park, Park House was built for the estate manager, and Park Cottages built to provide accommodation for workers.

Other changes resulted from attempts to improve growing conditions. To shelter the crops, windbreaks of Poplar trees were planted in 1947 but later many were removed when they became hosts to greenfly and other pests. Because drought was a persistent problem, freestanding drum-like reservoirs were installed on some holdings during the 1960s. But the problem of poor water supply worsened with the ever-increasing demands of intensive horticultural production, so the LSA constructed a butyl-lined reservoir for horticultural use only. The reservoir stored four million gallons of water drawn from five wells in Springhill Road and grateful growers breathed a sigh of relief, for they were at last confident of a continuous water supply. In earlier days Theta Smith, nee Messenger,

This Agreement is made the _sixteenth_ day of
June 19 7 1 BETWEEN THE LAND SETTLEMENT
ASSOCIATION LIMITED whose registered office is situate at 43 Cromwell
Road in the County of London (hereinafter called "the Association") as
agent for and on behalf of THE MINISTER OF AGRICULTURE
FISHERIES AND FOOD (hereinafter called "the Minister") the Association

acting by its Secretary WILLIAM NEWTON TAYLOR

of the one part and MRS. SADIE JOBLING

of 34, COOTES LANE, FEN DRAYTON, CAMBRIDGESHIRE

(hereinafter called "the Tenant") of the other part

WHEREAS:

(A) The property more particularly described in the First Schedule hereto
(hereinafter called "the Holding") is one of a group of holdings situate upon
the Minister's FEN DRAYTON
Estate (hereinafter called "the Estate")

(B) The Minister has appointed the Association as his agent to manage
on his behalf the said group of smallholdings situate on the Estate together
with other groups of smallholdings situate elsewhere in England (all of which
groups of smallholdings are hereinafter collectively referred to as "the Land
Settlement Smallholdings")

(C) The Minister has for the purpose of paragraph (C) of sub-section (4)
of Section 11 of the Agricultural Holdings Act 1948 as amended by the
Agriculture (Miscellaneous Provisions) Act 1949 and the Agriculture Act 1970
(the said Act of 1948 as subsequently amended by other enactments being
hereinafter called "the Act of 1948") approved a Scheme (hereinafter called "the
Scheme") which provides for the disposal of the produce of the Land Settlement
Smallholdings

(D) In pursuance of the Scheme the Minister has agreed to grant to the
Tenant and the Tenant has agreed to take from the Minister a tenancy of the
Holding upon the terms and conditions hereinafter set forth

NOW THIS AGREEMENT WITNESSETH AND IT IS HEREBY
AGREED as follows: —

PART I

PRELIMINARY

1. Definitions   1. IN this Agreement except where the context otherwise requires—

"PRODUCE" of the Holding includes all crops hay straw haulm fruit
vegetables plants cuttings seeds livestock poultry eggs manure and other
agricultural or horticultural produce of whatsoever kind produced grown or
kept upon the Holding

"MARKETABLE PRODUCE" of the Holding means all the produce of
the Holding except hay straw haulm root crops (not being root crops normally
grown for sale) and forage crops grown thereon and manure made or produced
thereon

"REQUISITE" for the Holding includes any building or erection (whether
a fixture or not) situate or intended to be situate upon the Holding and any
equipment implement tool livestock poultry eggs for setting plants seeds
fertilisers feeding stuffs or other goods for use on the Holding or in connection
with the cropping stocking or cultivation thereof or the grading packing or
marketing of any produce thereof

Sadie Jobling cultivating chrysanthemums at 34 Cootes Lane. She took over the tenancy of the smallholding after the death of her husband John and, when she retired, was followed by son Keith who became a third generation tenant.

had the unenviable task of warning them when the water was about to be turned off, which was often. In 1971 crops consumed 25 million gallons.

Outwitting the Managers

The outwitting of managers continued, I learned, throughout the history of the estate. Growers were tempted by ready money offered by greengrocers and wholesalers. But Maurice Lanchebury of Middleton Way discovered it was not worth the risk after getting his fingers burnt by fraudsters, who after gaining his trust, took lettuces and disappeared without paying for them. He thought others did very well out of the private selling. Some growers would secretly transport produce as far away as London. Theta explained that in earlier times she would hear vehicles moving out at night and returning hours later.

Some people traded outside the Association because of the better prices available, but less competent smallholders did so because they had debts and were desperate for money. This greatly annoyed those who kept to the rules and expressed to me a dislike of such doings. They said the organisation needed sufficient quantities passing through the packhouse to cover the costs of the scheme, and that selling produce outside the LSA put a greater burden on those who didn't. They were very critical of rulebreakers.

There was another possible source of dissatisfaction for tenants. They were given an annual bonus by the LSA according to the amount they spent in the stores and the quantity of produce put through the packhouse. One year Maurice Lanchebury for one, was extremely upset when he received nothing even though he had bought a large glasshouse through the Association. He was told it was because the estate had to subsidise the cost of closing the northern estates. This was quite a blow to him.

The LSA grower's average income fell in the 1960s, but rose in the early 1970's. In 1973, whereas an average farm worker's wage was £1,374 per annum, an L.S.A. tenant's average net income was £3,534. With Fen Drayton growers' average income amongst the highest in the Association, there was an air of optimism on the estate but could this last? Events were taking place that would present them with challenges including Britain's entry into the Common Market.

Diligence and hard work did not ensure a profitable outcome. Diseases, the vagaries of the weather and unpredictable events conspired to reduce profits. Maurice Lanchebury explained how the practice of farmers to burn stubble after the harvest (burning is now banned) produced sooty ash that descended into outdoor lettuces making them un-saleable, and also drifted inside the glasshouses. Philip Hamlett explained how growers attempted to remove the ash from chrysanthemums with domestic vacuum cleaners switched to low power. Lettuce crops could also be ruined when wind shattered glass fell into them, or hailstones shredded them, or when their leaves were burnt by cold winds. Unexpected cold weather snaps caused low demand for salads and little or no income for the growers, whereas heat waves caused high demand and high returns, but the growers could not meet that demand to take full advantage of it.

Treatments to combat pests and diseases, to which indoor plants were particularly susceptible, were costly. For example Scleratinia, a fungal disease which affected celery crops grown in the fenlands, spread to the estates where it lay dormant in the soil. To sterilise the soil with gas (metal bromide) cost £200 - £300 for each structure. Yet another outlay for the grower before there was a product to sell.

Smallholders helped each other through difficult times. For example, when Mr Frank Dale was ill a group of men cut his lettuces to save the crop, and when Pip Gill had a heart attack several tenants helped him by disbudding chrysanthemums for a month. At another time of need several tenants gathered the crops of a lady when her husband died suddenly. They did so although it became increasingly difficult for them to spare time to help others because of the increased size of their own production.

Adapting but losing the race

Because tomatoes weren't making money, growers like Maurice Lanchebury tried growing cucumbers which gave quite a good profit but were hard work. They were very heavy when carried twenty at a time. He also grew celery and made a good profit at first, but later had to contend with imports and new home competition, which included large quantities of celery grown by Greens of Soham. When watering their celery, to protect their skin from the celery tips which caused painful blisters, Maurice and his wife Jean arrayed themselves in hats and jackets and trousers over which they wore black bin bags tucked into Wellington boots. Most unpleasantly, the bin bags channelled water intended for the celery down into their boots.

The tenants, who saw they could both buy and sell products at better rates outside the organisation, judged it was not well run. In fact there was weakness at the top when strength was needed in the face of increasing competition, and the prevailing unsettled economic conditions nationally.

We have seen that LSA tenants had differing growing abilities and work ethics. Some of the disgruntled allowed less wise heads to influence their actions. Philip Hamlett explained how Siddlesham estate's growers

111

unilaterally staged a protest march inside J. Sainsbury's Chichester store, which they accused of depriving English growers of their livelihood by buying imported produce. Philip was embarrassed by the demonstration because Sainsburys had purchased £450,000 worth of LSA produce that year. But the men's discontent was a reflection of the increasing disquiet felt in the glasshouse industry and in the country as a whole. The growers' livelihoods would be badly affected by circumstances beyond their control.

It was a time of high inflation, and a fuel crisis. To combat this Ted Heath, Conservative Prime Minister, introduced the Three Day Week to conserve fuel. This came into force on 31 December 1973. Earlier in the year he had enrolled Britain in the Common Market. The growers wondered how it would affect them. Jim Scutt did not stay long enough to find out. Doris had had enough of life on the Cootes Lane smallholding and persuaded him to give notice to quit. They left the estate in 1975 after 34 years but were to learn later that they might have been better off, financially, if they had not done so.

The Common Market & other Upsets

By 1973-75, as we have seen, the growers were expanding their glass area. Also, encouraged by government grants of 40 per cent, they converted their glasshouses to cheap oil heating to match those of the Common Market glass industry. Almost immediately there was a dramatic rise in the price of oil. Then the growers experienced the unprecedented long hot summer of 1976, which caused a glut of tomatoes and tons had to be dumped. Nevertheless, the average income increased until crop year 1979. It was also the year the Conservatives (who were against the concept of tied cottages) came to power. The LSA's 1979/80 Annual Report was brought to the attention of Peter Walker, Minister of Agriculture. It showed that the tenants' Average Net Farm Income had been reduced that year by 6.7%.

In 1979, because of the high cost of heating, growers delayed their planting programme. This caused higher peaks in the production of lettuce and tomatoes. The high tomato yields, increased still further by another uncharacteristically hot summer, had to compete during the critical months of July to September with tomatoes entering the English market from the government-subsidised Dutch growers. Once again tons of first class tomatoes were destroyed and then, during the winter of 1979, the price of oil increased seventeen times. Higher oil costs meant higher glasshouse-heating costs, higher costs of non-returnable plastic packaging because it

112

was derived from oil, and higher transport costs, which made it expensive to export celery to Germany. An unusually warm spring followed which led to the first ever Spring lettuce glut. Lettuces were so unprofitable to market that growers ploughed them into the ground. On one occasion, said Ian Ruggles of Middleton Way, he received only one penny per dozen after marketing and packaging costs were deducted.

It is April 1980 at 44 Middleton Way, and Ian and Edna Ruggles are harvesting the lettuces they had planted between November and December. Because of the difficult economic climate they made little profit on them. In spite of the considerable difficulties he and other growers faced, Ian was grateful that the LSA had provided him with the opportunity to acquire a smallholding.

There were other problems. For example, Ian was distraught when he lost a chrysanthemum crop potentially worth £10,000 on the 1980 Christmas market. It was destroyed overnight when the oil supply to his glasshouse heating system froze. Then returns from early glasshouse celery, a reliable crop for LSA growers, were badly affected when Guernsey's tomato growers, also faced by Dutch government-subsidised competition, began to produce celery too. There was further competition from abroad as ever larger refrigerated lorries were able to bring produce from greater distances and to add to the growers' problems, record rates of interest were being charged. They were disastrous for those who had invested heavily in glass.

113

Some growers obtained further loans to help them get through difficult years, but their debts mounted. In 1981, five Fen Drayton growers were forced out of business with others also vulnerable. They were not alone with their problems. In 1980 the NFU created a National Glasshouse

Celery grown by Roger Robinson in the 1970's

In the 1970's at No. 8 Mill Road.
On the left Derek Robinson's son Paul is
cutting celery with the aid of paid help.

Survival Committee, and in 1981 it organised a protest march in London, mainly about Dutch imports. Figures produced by the Cambridge University Department of Land Economy for the glasshouse industry in that year, showed that nurseries in the Cambridge area were losing between £13,000 and £14,000 per 2.4 acres (a hectare). Philip Hamlett took over Fen Drayton that year. He said it was getting into "very bad water" and there was a general air of uncertainty.

Increasingly dissatisfied, LSA tenants lobbied Members of Parliament and Peter Walker and Francis Pym visited Fen Drayton with Earl Ferrers in February 1982 to discuss the problems the tenants were faced with.

Even successful efficient growers found it difficult to make a profit. Roger Robinson, like some other growers, had made a good living for 15 – 18 years but felt helpless when everything seemed beyond his control. He, who had served on many committees, resigned from the LSA Executive committee in October 1982 and gave notice he was quitting his holding because of poor profits. He would run a Post Office instead although he had been at Mill Road for 21 years.

Other tenants accused the Association of mismanagement and complained about the unfair competition of the government-subsidised Dutch glasshouse industry, and they demanded that the central marketing and packaging system should be returned to estate level. The LSA's representatives, including a talented new chief executive only appointed in 1981, were in discussions with Ministry officials in many late night meetings. Hours were spent considering solutions but Peter Walker rejected plans to save the organisation. He had come to a decision. He had decided that the future of the estates lay in the formation of individual estate co-operatives, organised and controlled by the growers themselves.

The unique experiment would end

Chapter 6

1982 – 2007 The End of the Experiment

On 1 December 1982, growers listened to radios or watched their televisions with disbelief as the Minister of Agriculture announced that the LSA smallholding scheme was to end. He stated that all the estates would be sold, all services would be withdrawn, and that the central marketing system would cease to exist at the end of March 1983. Earlier that day, I was told, a group of Fen Drayton's workers had been hastily summoned to a meeting because one had received ominous leaked news. The men emerged from the meeting lighting up cigarettes and looking grim. All LSA jobs were to be terminated on 3 March and all accounting departments would be closed.

Everyone received the news without warning. The three Senior Estate Managers learned that same day that they had only four months in which to close down all the services, a seemingly impossible task. Philip Hamlett said the closure date was set for Maundy Thursday, the busiest lettuce-marketing day of the year. He asked who was going to account for the money and deal with all the other problems. For example, who would harvest the half of Abington Estate that he was farming, and he questioned that there would be enough time allowed for tenants to make new arrangements.

Perhaps Peter Walker had not read the Tenancy Agreement. It stipulated that tenants must give the Association twelve months' notice to vacate their holdings. Aggrieved tenants felt they should have at least that amount of time to readjust, so the Minister extended the deadline to December 1983.

He solved another problem, that of the lifelong tenancy agreements, by offering the tenants the opportunity to buy their holding. Some had long hoped for this and the offer was extended to those, like Roger Robinson, who were already working their notice. But it was too late for others who had, due to mounting debts or ill health, severed their contracts because the Minister had continued to say that it was not Ministry policy to sell up, and of course Jim and Doris Scutt too had left their holding too soon and missed the chance to buy their house at a very favourable price.

Although shocked by the news the Lancheburys were partly pleased by it. They had felt very low as they watched the organisation going down-hill, and shared the feelings of despondency and even desperation of others who, like the Kent-Ledgers of Middleton Way, were "working their socks off for fourteen hours a day". They were only just keeping their heads above water so were optimistic that they would be better off if part of a co-operative, and gain more control over their lives. Their hopes were put to the test when they became members of a new consortium named Fen Drayton Growers.

Fen Drayton Growers needed a packhouse. Partly financed by the Ministry of Agriculture and "Food from Britain" (a partly government funded marketing organisation), it was built close to the A14 main road and opened in June 1984 by John MacGregor, a Junior Agriculture Minister. The Consortium's produce from just fifteen Fen Drayton Growers, plus some from other estates, was marketed under the name of "English Village Salads", through "Home Grown Salads" (HGS). HGS, based in Kent, supplied produce to stores such as Marks and Spencer, J Sainsbury and Fine Fare. The consortium was disbanded after only five years partly because there were no replacements for retiring growers and partly because no one was willing to replace the outgoing manager. I learned that even as members of the consortium some growers could not see it was in their own interests to work for the whole group.

The packhouse built for the new consortium of Fen Drayton Growers Ltd. It was sold when the consortium disbanded after trading for only five years. Because the smallholdings became privately owned and the LSA was disbanded, younger people had difficulty getting a foot on the smallolding ladder, so there were no new growers to replace those that reached retirement age.

The experience of the post LSA co-operatives would suggest that life without the LSA was not easy. Very few are still in existence. Pip Gill, LSA Propagating Manager and then chrysanthemum growing tenant, told me the LSA had been like a cocoon and he regretted its passing.

Effects on the village

The dismantling of the LSA organisation changed Fen Drayton. The Central Farm (Middleton Farm) and its outbuildings was razed to the ground. And so, there in the heart of the village, the busy activities of packing and grading of salads by local people, and the bustle and noise of farm and delivery vehicles and supermarket lorries had disappeared. The manager, the advisers and the accountant were gone, the flower handling facilities were gone, the packhouse and the great propagating glasshouse were gone and so was the Village Hall. All replaced by high-density housing containing strangers.

119

 **Ekins, Dilley & Handley**

Centenary House HUNTINGDON Tel: Huntingdon (0480) 56171

By Direction of R. A. & R. J. Robinson

CATALOGUE

**Dispersal sale by Auction of
Market Garden Machinery and Equipment**

To be held at
8 Mill Road,
Fen Drayton
Cambridgeshire

Saturday January 29th 1983 at 10.30 a.m.

VIEW: Morning of Sale

Light Refreshments available

Further Enquiries
of
Huntingdon Office
Ref: PL/5R626

A superior Village Hall with tennis courts and a bowling green was built on former LSA land, and in the garden of Fen Drayton House five large houses were built with others close by. The former estate houses and smallholdings immediately began to acquire new images as owners stamped them with their own personalities. Some are now difficult to recognise as settlement houses: the process continues.

In 2007 only two holdings out of the original 52 are involved in commercial salad production besides the several in Oak Tree Road bought by an Italian whose business, based at No 18, is called Stubbins Marketing Ltd. In the post-LSA era he began an enterprise with its roots in market gardening but his salads are produced on an industrial scale under many acres of glass.

With salad growing on the holdings almost a bygone occupation, there has been much experimentation, and new enterprises come and go. No. 2 Mill Road was an Alpine Nursery for a while then became Thimblemill Nurseries Toy & Plant Sales. This too had ceased trading by July 2005 and a new owner is offering a landscape gardening service and is creating demonstration show gardens. At 3 Mill Road a Mr Tacchi began a Wholesale Tree Nursery business, then K. J. Willis adapted it to sell shrubs and bedding plants. Holding No. 25 Springhill Road, has had a varied life. It became a Livery Stable, then a farm animal sanctuary, and later horse paddocks which also feature elsewhere on the estate. Recently Shetland ponies grazed on a Middleton way holding, and several holdings provided grazing for sheep and lambs. I was heartened when a goat stepped out of a shed. Other holdings are now ornamental gardens or resemble littered waste ground. From a good many the saleable glasshouses have been removed but others have greenhouses listing to one side full of weeds or completely submerged beneath thickets of brambles. Some holdings have been divided, or amalgamated to make larger units, and speculators hope non-agricultural development will eventually be allowed. They may well be disappointed if South Cambridgeshire District Council's suggested plans bear fruit. These can be seen in the Local Development Framework Site Specific Policies Development Plan Document.
...
2. HOUSING

POLICY SP/9 Fen Drayton Former Land Settlement Association Estate.
"Within the former Land Settlement Association Site at Fen Drayton, as defined on the Proposals Map, where it can be demonstrated that buildings (excluding glass houses) are no longer needed for agricultural purposes, planning permission for

1988, the new Village Hall, sitting on land previously owned by the LSA, provides better facilities than the old one. Nevertheless, it is unlikely to be host to as many jolly occasions as was the old hall now that the growing community has all but disappeared.

An aerial view of Fen Drayton in 1994. At the top can be seen smallholdings in Middleton way, Mill Road and Cootes Lane. Left of centre, new housing has replaced Middleton Farm, the LSA's Central Farm complex, and the Village Hall. Above centre to the right in Cootes Lane is the new Village Hall awaiting its tennis courts and bowling green and to its left is the modern village school. Just right of centre Fen Drayton House hides behind a group of trees. It was turned into well-appointed flats and sold by the LSA.

change of use or redevelopment of existing buildings will be permitted for on site experimental or other ground-breaking forms of sustainable living provided that development would not occupy a larger footprint than existing buildings.

.... In view of the area's history and its current appearance, form and character this policy will allow it to evolve as a positive experimental test-bed for new forms of sustainable living. "

The document appears to indicate that Fen Drayton is once more to play its part in an experiment.

It seems that as a result of the changes since the sale, the atmosphere of the village may not feel as friendly as previously. One resident explained that when she works in her garden people no longer stop to pass the time of day and there are many new faces and commuters.

It is also interesting to note that the former way of life of the early incomers has also disappeared. The last of the great shipyards, Swan Hunter, closed recently, and all the hundreds of collieries of the North East have gone and with them the jobs they provided, and the slag heaps and the grime, and the soot, and rows and rows of back-to-back housing. They have been replaced with country parks and industrial estates and new housing. Many of the remaining houses have been modernised and double-glazed and support satellite dishes but some, nevertheless, look very dispirited. Surviving pit wheels are in museums or painted blue and propped in flowerbeds. But gratifyingly, numerous colliery bands survive and Houghton-le-Spring still holds an annual Festival. Durham's annual Gala also continues with thousands attending and joining in the celebrations but their numbers are far fewer in the aftermath of all the pit closures.

The closure of the Land Settlement Scheme in 1983 was followed by litigation. It was claimed that the Minister for Agriculture should not have withdrawn the various central services. The case reached the House of Lords where it was decided that only in the area of marketing did the Ministry have an on-going obligation to the growers, but as no-one qualified, nobody made a claim. Then, about half of the Association's ex-tenants sued the Minister for between £25,000,000 - £38,000,000 for alleged mismanagement (the figures were never specified). The case was concluded in July 1991 in an out-of-court settlement. Each side had to pay their own costs.

Philip Hamlett, who acted in the capacity of a consultant reporting to the Ministry of Agriculture after the sale, was extremely unhappy about the out-of-court settlement. He claims many false allegations were made through an Expert Witness and that the former tenants had no idea of the accusations being made on their behalf; this was corroborated by a grower.

Philip said he had sought to give a realistic assessment of potential tenants' prospects and thought the result very unfair to many of the staff who had worked so hard and conscientiously to aid the growers. One litigant's wife from Middleton Way told me she felt their grievances were justified and that they were entitled to the money. Another is still very annoyed that the Manager allowed her husband to take on a holding in 1976, but I do wonder if he would have needed a crystal ball to predict what was to come. Another late arrival, a tenant from 1976, told me the LSA let them down.

The out of court settlement of £6.5 million, which was actually £2.9 million plus interest, created bad feeling between former tenants because non-litigants were ineligible for compensation. Philip Hamlett tried to acquire a share for them too but was opposed. One non-litigant said it left a nasty taste in the mouth because the settlement was made without regard to whether or not a particular individual deserved compensation. Another agreed, he said they had been led to believe they would be treated equally if there was a pay out. The reason some growers had not sued was because they were not eligible for legal aid.

In spite of the troubles, the following quotation would tend to support the view that much of the LSA's work had been a success. In 1975, K. J. McCready wrote in "The Land Settlement Association:- Its History and Present Form".

> *"... the main emphasis must be placed on the fact that the initial sociological experiment has survived through forty years of almost constant change. This indicates not only the basic validity of the original concept but also a remarkable ability on the part of the successive management teams to adapt and adopt ideas in the face of considerable political involvement..."*

Finally, the Head Office of the LSA at 43 Cromwell Road, London, was sold, and the proceeds used to establish a charitable trust administered by the Royal Agricultural Benevolent Society based at 27 West Way, Oxford. Its main aims are to aid any ex-LSA tenants or staff who fall into dire straits and to provide any deserving cases with assistance towards an agricultural or horticultural education.

Chapter 7
Conclusion
A worthwhile Experiment

During the severe industrial depression following the First World War the socially conscious, who included the Quakers, the Carnegie Trustees and Sir Malcolm Stewart among many others, laboured to ease the distress of the destitute and desperate families living in areas of industrial high unemployment. Out of the Quakers' substantial experimental work with allotment schemes for the unemployed, grew a more ambitious possible solution to unemployment - Land Settlement. Just over fifty years ago a unique experiment began and unemployed miners and shipyard workers like Jack Jobling, Bob Carter, Tim Foster and Tom Pope accepted the offer of a completely new way of life on land far away from their home areas.

Fen Drayton's inhabitants, like those of other parishes chosen to be hosts to the new Land Settlement Scheme, saw their parish transformed overnight with the arrival of the men from the north. The depressed village of Fen Drayton was enlivened by the newcomers and its population more than doubled, all much to the amazement of village families including the Wilderspins, the Ingles, the Giddings, Mr Culpin the blacksmith, Mr Househam the milkman, and Pa and Ma Green at the Three Tuns.

Over the years the villagers observed continual change in the landscape and the LSA community. This was because the LSA continually adapted its policies as political and economic events forced a re-think on the purpose of the estates. The village often lost smallholders who decided to move to other ventures, but gained new hopefuls wishing to take advantage of the special opportunity on offer. The estate was a significant factor in the villagers' lives and I think, overall, they realised that Fen Drayton would have been the poorer without it.

The inhabitants of the estate today barely resemble those of earlier times because their lives are so varied. In 2007 only three of the people who are cultivating holdings commercially remain from the LSA era, and only one of them is linked to the first settlers. Neville Gill, the grandson of Bob Carter the Sunderland shipyard worker, continues to grow flowers on his two holdings in Cootes Lane.

125

Would the originators of the scheme have considered their efforts worthwhile? I would think so. Although the original pressing need, and overwhelming reason for the creation of the estates disappeared in a relatively short time, I think they would have been pleased to have provided so many people with a fresh start in life, and be justifiably proud of the part the estates played both nationally and locally. Perhaps it needs the same courage to approach a similar problem today. Unbelievably, in the Jobling family's home area in Sunderland, some men have been jobless for many years in spite of regeneration investment schemes.

Of those for whom the scheme was created, a large number did not succeed in becoming smallholders, but Jack Jobling, Tim Foster and Tom Pope were among those who did, remaining on their holdings until retirement age. Bob Carter was among those who gave up the smallholding way of life, but like quite a few of them gained alternative employment in the south. But often it was the children of the settlers who benefited most, for mainly they had an enjoyable, well fed, country childhood and many of them went on to obtain good jobs and careers.

My intention when writing this book has been to try to illuminate the fascinating world of the people whose lives were touched by a unique experiment. I hope I have done the story justice.

As to how I would reply, if asked whether Mr Watson, who so long ago guided my attention to Fen Drayton, made the right decision when he left its estate to set up a garden centre at Staunton Harold, I can't be sure. It would appear that he was one of those who used his holding as a stepping stone, and as his expanding garden centre appeared to be highly successful, it seems likely that he did make the correct choice.

Further Reading

CLARKE, PETER, 'Cooperative Working and the Land Settlement Scheme (LSA): A Historical Perspective', *The Yearbook of Agricultural Cooperation* (London, 1982).

DEARLOVE, PAMELA, The Effect of the Policies of the Land Settlement Association upon Fen Drayton, Cambridgeshire 1935-88, *Local History Society Review*, NS, 1-3 (Cambridge, 1992-4).

DEARLOVE, PAMELA, 'Fen Drayton, Cambridgeshire: An Estate of the Land Settlement Association', in J. Thirsk, (ed.), *The English Rural Landscape* (Oxford, 2000, pb edn., Rural England, Oxford 2002).

FRY, MARY, *Friends Lend a Hand Alleviating Unemployment* (London, 1947).

KITCHEN, FRED, E. J., *Settlers in England* (London, 1947).

Land Settlement Association, *Illustrations of the Work of the Land Settlement Association* (London, 1937).

McCREADY, K. J., *The Land Settlement Association: Its History and Present Form* (London, 1974).

Ministry of Agriculture, Fisheries, and Food, *Departmental Committee of Inquiry into Statutory Smallholdings*, Chaired by Professor M. J. Wise, Final Report (London, 1967).

The Full-time Smallholding Estates developed by the LSA.

Abington*
New House Farm, Great Abington, Cambridgeshire

Andover+
Little Park Farm, Andover, Hampshire

Broadwath+
Broadwath Farm, Heads Nook, Nr Carlisle, Cumberland

Chawston*
Chawston Manor. Chawston, and Rookery Farm, Wyboston, Bedfordshire

Crofton+
Crofton Hall, Thursby, Nr Carlisle, Cumberland

Dalston+
Dalston Hall, Lingey Close Head, Dalston, Carlisle, Cumberland

Duxbury
Farnworth House Estate, Duxbury, Lancashire

Elmesthorpe+
Church Farm, Elmesthorpe, Nr Earl Shilton, Leicestershire

Fen Drayton*
Middleton Farm, Fen Drayton, Cambridgeshire

Foxash*
Ardleigh, Essex

Fulney*
Dairy Farm, Lower Fulney, Nr Spalding, Lincolnshire

Harrowby+
Harrowby Hall, Nr Grantham, Lincolnshire

Newbourne*
Newbourn Hall, Nr Woodbridge, East Suffolk

Newent*
The Scarr, Newent, Gloucestershire

Oxcroft+
Shuttlewood, Nr Chesterfield, Derbyshire

Potton*
Home Farm, Potton, Bedfordshire

Sidlesham*
Keynor Farm, (also Fletchers and Streetend Farms), Sidlesham, Chichester, Sussex

Snaith*
West Bank Farm, Carlton, Snaith, Nr Goole, Yorkshire

Stannington+
Moor Farm, Stannington, Morpeth, Northumberland

Yeldham
The Change, Great Yeldham, Essex

* Listed in LSA Annual Report 1979/80
+ Estates still functioning in 1966 but recommended for early withdrawal from the scheme

Duxbury and Yeldham were in the scheme only until shortly after the war.

"L.S.A Estates were widely separated, as far apart from the Solway Firth to the English Channel and from Suffolk to the Bristol Channel". (Professor Wise)

Additional Caption - lower picture page 60

The children are listening to Mr Kidd, acting Head Master, at Fen Drayton School in 1940 (see page 60).

Lhs group, 2nd row, Jack Wilderspin peers between two boys.
Front row, l to r: Billy Laverick from Sunderland, and unknown.

Centre group, 2nd row, l to r: Alan Crick from Durham. and unknown.
Front row, l to r: unknown, George Foster and Tim Foster, from Page Bank, Durham.

Rhs group, 3rd row, Connie Pope, from the Rhondda,
2nd row, ? Gladys Nutall from Thornley, Durham.
Front row, Theta Messenger from Esh Winning, Durham.

During the war the over eleven year olds were not allowed to make the journey to Swavesey School because it was considered too dangerous for them to do so. Instead they swelled the numbers at Fen Drayton School.

Additional Picture Acknowledgements

Page 15 : Pithead allotments Pontypridd- "by courtesy of The Society of Friends"

Page 12 : Muddy Back Lane, Page Bank - ref 22448 and
Page 13 : Houghton-Le-Spring hunger marchers 1936 - ref 22421
by courtesy of "BEAMISH The North of England Open Air Museum.

Page 21 : Public sale notice - "by permission of the Syndics of Cambridge University Library" : reference No. Maps.PSQ.19.473

Page 101 : Aerial View of Fen Drayton (1972), BNK 89 - "by courtesy of Cambridge University Unit for Landscape Modelling -Air photograph library"

Page 122 : Aerial View of Fen Drayton (1994) - "by courtesy of Cambridge Evening News"

Index

R